DOUBLE

Also by Cameron Stracher

The Laws of Return

DOUBLE BILLING

Lies, and the Pursuit of a Swivel Chair

Cameron Stracher

Quill
William Morrow
New York

It is the policy of William Morrow and Company, Inc., and its imprints and affiliates, recognizing the importance of preserving what has been written, to print the books we publish on acid-free paper, and we exert our best efforts to that end.

The Library of Congress has cataloged a previous edition of this title.

Library of Congress Cataloging-in-Publication Data

Stracher, Cameron.
Double billing : a young lawyer's tale of greed, sex, lies,
and the pursuit of a swivel chair / Cameron Stracher.—1st ed.
p.   cm.
ISBN 0-688-14759-3 (alk. paper)
1. Corporate lawyers—New York (State)—New York.   2. Practice of
law—New York (State)—New York.   I. Title.
KF299.I5S77   1998   98-8092
346.73'066'092—dc21   CIP
Paperback ISBN 0-688-17222-9

Printed in the United States of America

First Quill Edition 1999

5   6   7   8   9   10

BOOK DESIGN BY BERNARD KLEIN

www.williammorrow.com

For my parents and for Simon

Author's Note

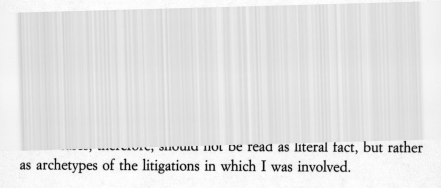

..., therefore, should not be read as literal fact, but rather as archetypes of the litigations in which I was involved.

Acknowledgments

DOUBLE

I Fought the Law

September.

I wake to the alarm clock's pummeling. Stumbling from bed, my eyelids glued like old wallpaper, I slap haphazardly at the snooze button. It eludes my hand like a skittering insect. Finally, in desperation, I knock the clock from the nightstand, silencing its warbling on the cold, rock-hard floor. What time is it? Time to rise; time to shine.

In the bathroom, while I wait for the hot water, I examine my face in the mirror. The lines around my lips have deepened. My hair has thinned and even grayed. I am twenty-six years old, practically ancient. What I know could fill a book; what I don't would fill the world.

Soon, steam fogs the glass. The pipes clank. I shower, shampoo, and shave. Dab myself with lotions, ointments, and creams. Wrap myself in towels and tissues. Shielded from the elements, I pad back to the bedroom to dress.

Everything smells of fresh paint and soap: the apartment, my clothes, this job. I am not unexcited. Nervous, perhaps, and a bit apprehensive. I've never held a full-time job before. I've been a waiter, pizza deliverer, disc jockey, to name a few, but none of these professions seemed substantial, real. I was biding time until *life* arrived.

I walk to the kitchenette in my underwear and white shirt. The shirt is starched so stiffly it hangs in panels from my shoulders. I had to bend the cuffs to button them. I pour another cup of coffee, careful to hold it far from my chest. My nerves thrum like piano wire.

It feels like the first day of school. The same churning in the stomach. The same unfamiliar routine. New clothes, new books, new friends. A bus stop to route out. I will be beaten by a bully, ignored by the teacher, and abandoned in the back of study hall.

I fold my shirt into my pants. Loop my belt through the loops. Mash my feet into my black wingtips. Tie and untie and retie my tie. At nine o'clock I race around the small apartment shutting off appliances: coffeemaker, air conditioner, television, iron. I switch off the lights, grab the unread newspaper, and skip out the door.

The Law crooks one finger and beckons.

I graduated Harvard Law School at the beginning of a decade of diminished expectations. The stock market had crashed, staggered, and recovered, but the economy was still in free fall. "Downsizing," the media had dubbed it. College students were rushing to law school in desperate numbers. The recently unemployed, the bored, the fearful were joining them. Academics warned of a "brain drain." Politicians feared a "litigation explosion." Lawyers worried about the competition.

Despite the souring economy, my classmates had all found jobs: clerkships with federal judges, prosecutors in district attorneys' offices, legal counsel to public interest organizations. The vast majority, however, were heading into private practice, the bulk of them to big firms in New York City.

In the last decades there has been a spectacular increase in the number of lawyers. There are now nearly one million in the United States, about the same as the federal prison population. Although more lawyers work as solo practitioners, the number in group practices has grown steadily since World War II, while the ranks of solo practitioners have shrunk. The growth among large firms, those with more than fifty lawyers, has been dramatic: the percentage of lawyers in such firms doubled during the 1980s. The increase at the large firms has come .....

..... to workers and consumers expanded, and as corporations bought, sold, and reorganized themselves with stunning alacrity, the demand for lawyers multiplied. More lawyers also created a need for more lawyers. As my criminal-law professor once joked: a lawyer comes to a small town to set up a practice. He spends his days twiddling his thumbs, doing the odd real estate closing or uncontested divorce. He lives a lazy, low-budget life. One day, another lawyer moves to town. Suddenly, they both have more work than they can handle.

Most of the largest firms in the world (and large law firms are a distinctly American phenomenon) have their biggest offices in New York City. Firms with more than two hundred lawyers spread over multiple floors in a single building are not uncommon. Add to this the number of secretaries, paralegals, librarians, word-processing staff, messengers, and other support staff, and these firms resemble small campuses connected by elevators.

At Harvard very few law students begin their first year intending to work for one of the large firms. Most of my classmates professed interest in signing up with employers like the ACLU or the Center for Constitutional Rights—liberal organizations that defend a woman's right to choose, equal access to political representation, free speech. But by their second year, when interviewers from the biggest firms swarm onto campus waving stacks of cash, dinners at expensive restaurants, and nights at a posh hotel, few are idealistic enough to resist.

It begins like this: your roommate asks who you're interviewing with. You tell him you don't plan to work for a firm; you intend to fight to keep Greenland green. He tells you you're crazy. You should at least sign up for an on-campus interview, submit your résumé, see what happens. You have nothing to lose. You're interviewing for a summer job—a "summer associate." Everyone knows these jobs are like going to camp. You make a lot of money, go out for expensive lunches, and go home early. At the end of the summer, you return to law school with a permanent offer tucked in your pocket like a piece of cheese to nibble on through your final year.

In the decade of diminished expectations, employers still flocked to Harvard. While interviewers dwindled and disappeared at other law schools, the competition remained fierce for graduates of Harvard and comparable schools. The simple laws of supply and demand, the only principle I remembered from college economics, worked in our favor. As law firms grew, the number of Harvard graduates stayed the same.

I have worked with graduates from many different law schools. I have spoken with lawyers from varied legal backgrounds. And I can report that the job search experiences of students outside the so-called elite law schools—Harvard, Yale, Stanford, Columbia, Michigan, Chicago—and perhaps a half-dozen more, are very different from mine. At most schools, law firms rarely come to campus to interview. If they do, they are interested only in the very top of the class. Students scramble to find jobs, writing letters to everyone they know and to names plucked off a letterhead. Many, if not most, are unemployed upon graduation. In the late 1980s, when law firms actually fired lawyers, they were the first to be let go. A friend of mine who graduated at the top of his class at the University of Iowa was fired from his prestigious New York firm only six months after he started work. The firm explained that his needs were incompatible with its. Read: You went to Iowa; firing you won't hurt our recruiting efforts at Yale.

But at Harvard, if you left your résumé with the career counseling center, someone would call you later that day to schedule an on-campus interview. It was not unusual for students to have twenty on-campus int

After the on-campus interview, the phone would ring. That pasty-faced man who droned insistently about his asbestos case would like to know if I wanted to fly down to New York at his firm's expense for another round of interviews. I tried to remember what I had said that would interest him in me, but soon convinced myself that he was actually quite perceptive and saw through my glazed expression to the personable, intelligent, and quick-witted soul beneath. The firm's "recruiting coordinator" booked the flight and made a reservation at the Waldorf Astoria. "Will that be all right?" she asked. I had never stayed at the Waldorf, let alone any hotel in Manhattan. How could I refuse?

Of course, not every on-campus interview led to a "fly-back." Every fly-back did not lead to a job offer. But I soon found that I could not make all the fly-backs I had accepted, and certainly could not accept all the summer jobs I was offered. I was not at the top of my class. I had not made law review—the prestigious law journal edited by students. However, my experiences were not unique. Even today, as I write these words, Harvard students still entertain more job offers than they could possibly accept.

They are the lucky ones.

The subway station is thick with heat. The haze and humidity of a summer in the city have accumulated below the surface like a poisonous gas. I scramble for a token while an express train bombs down the disintegrating rails. Plaster flakes from overhead. Water drips through rusted metal.

I push through the ancient turnstile and step onto a piece of chewing gum. As I try to scrape it from my shoe, a homeless man approaches and asks for a quarter. I hop away from him and bounce against a support column.

Sweat beads along my forehead, trickles down my temples, dampens the rim of my collar. The station is at least ninety degrees and airless, and I am wearing a long-sleeved shirt buttoned to the neck, a tie, and a wool suit. Who ordained this dress code? Why do we obey it? I look down the platform at other men and women who stand coolly, reading *The New York Times*, the *Daily News*, *The Wall Street Journal,* pages creased perfectly into bite-sized panels. A mad evolution has bred this implacable race of city dwellers. Now I, too, must learn how to adapt and survive.

The train shrieks into the station, brakes screeching, asbestos on steel. In contrast to the general dinginess, the train shines like a child's toy. The doors open and a wall of beleaguered faces stare back at me. I couldn't slip between them with a shoehorn. I dash to the next set of open doors, but the same weary faces glare out. Finally, as a pinging tone sounds, I fling myself into the can of sardines amid general grunting and elbow-jabbing. The doors close. The train lurches. Nothing to breathe but everyone's exhaust.

Here we go.

Crowley & Cavanaugh occupied the top eight floors in a thirty-five-story skyscraper in midtown Manhattan, a few blocks from Grand Central Station. Like many other law firms, C & C broke away from the Wall Street area in the mid-1980s when practices were booming and space downtown was tight. Before the move, it was not uncommon for lawyers to share offices until their third or fourth year at the firm. With the fat profits from their practice, however, C & C spread their hefty bottoms northward, trading the prestige of a Wall Street address for the prestige of rosewood and marble conference rooms, teal and burnished aluminum reception areas, cherry floors, terra-cotta tiles, chintz draperies. Though still referred to as a "Wall Street law firm," its client list comprising financial institutions and mega-corporations, C & C was now miles north of that fabled and denuded land.

The move had ……… ……… …

……… …… unobstructed views of Manhattan and generous allowances for office furniture and decorations.

Light and space. Like some principle of relativity, the more you had, the faster you were moving. Partners had the corner offices, the ones on the higher floors, the large southern exposures. Associates had offices with windows and played a frantic game of musical chairs when colleagues departed and their offices became available. Paralegals dwelled in the interior offices, two to a room. Secretaries were grouped in threes and fours in "stations" near their bosses, their faces visible to all who passed in the hallway, a four-foot wall obstructing only their computers. And in the inner circle, airless and lightless, clanking with the machine drone of copiers, smelling of toner and grease, crowded with boxes and files, dwelled the messengers and file clerks. While the lawyers and paralegals had doors, and the secretaries at least had cubicles, these unfortunate denizens of the middle world were without a nameplate, a telephone, a place to sit. They leaned against bookshelves and hovered near the monstrous machines as the gears spat out paper like flies.

The gender and complexion of C & C changed, too, as one moved inward. Almost all the partners were male and white. Associates were mostly white with a sprinkling of Asian, a dash of Latin, and several African Americans. Men still outnumbered women, especially among the senior associates. The secretaries were evenly divided between white women who tended to live in the outer boroughs of New York—Staten Island, Queens, Brooklyn—and black women who lived in the Bronx. The inner circle was composed almost entirely of young, black men.

The rare exception to these Dante-esque circles was the word-processing center. On the thirty-third floor, a shadowy blue-lit world of struggling artists, dancers, singers, and actors worked odd hours, nights, and weekends, generating the documents lawyers had scribbled and revised. A lawyer could mark up—"redline"—a one-hundred-page merger agreement, leave it with Word Processing at ten o'clock at night, and when she returned at nine the next morning it would be on her desk, revised, proofread, and bound. The word processors could come and go as they chose, quit on a whim, leave for a tour. C & C was not their entire existence; it was a job that paid the bills while they pursued their passions. Life, their real life, was elsewhere.

In law firm parlance, everyone but the lawyers was "support staff," camels loaded with provisions for a trek across the desert. One or two might fall in the heat, their bodies forgotten by the roadside. You hated to lose a good one. But at the end of the journey it was the lawyers who spun their hours into gold. The support staff drank their share at the oasis, then saddled up for the long ride home. It was a long ride home.

I am disgorged into a labyrinthine warren somewhere beneath Grand Central Station. Though I worked at C & C last summer, I have never commuted from the West Side, and without a compass or divining rod I wander randomly past the small unventilated shops that line the marbled hallways. I follow a stream of business people toward an exit sign, up an escalator, and then out a door onto an avenue. Uptown? Downtown? I have no clue where, in the maze of midtown Manhattan, I am.

Finally, I see a sign for Vanderbilt Avenue. Another sign tells me I am at the Forty-third Street corner. I have emerged at the wrong end of Grand Central. I race up Vanderbilt, across the street, and out onto Park. Though C & C's building has a Park Avenue address, it sits three buildings off Park, its address a function of tax breaks and political patronage.

Despite the video cameras, four hulking security guards, and a sign that commands all visitors to sign in, I slip by unchallenged, to

How did I get here?

I first arrived at Crowley & Cavanaugh as a summer associate. Following my second year of law school, like most of my classmates, I ventured to New York for the ritual summer with a large firm. There were thirty-eight of us, twelve from Harvard. We arrived around Memorial Day and stayed through August. We were paid the same salary as first-year associates—$85,000 a year—and given a $2,500 "bonus" to help with the expense of moving to New York for a summer. C & C also provided us with a list of apartments to sublet and offered to pay the broker's fee if we used one. I found an apartment off Lexington Avenue with my law school roommate, Julia Baker, and her boyfriend, Tom Dooley, a freelance journalist whom Julia had met at Stanford and who was looking for a job in New York.

What little I knew of New York law firms, I knew from Julia. Her older brother, Evan, was a senior associate at one of the most prominent firms in the city. Lawyers at this firm were reputed to be brilliant, eccentric, and workaholics. My grandmother toiled in a sweatshop, but she was paid by the piece; Evan billed by the hour.

Julia was tall, strawberry-haired, rail thin. Her father, a cardiologist, taught in the medical school at the University of Iowa. I learned this little bit of family background in the ten minutes before our first law school class, Contracts, as we sat fidgeting in our assigned seats. Sitting beside her that first day was, I hope, the closest I'll ever come to combat. Five minutes into the class, a shell landed next to me in the shape of a question from our Contracts professor.

Our Contracts professor was rumored to be the model for Professor Perini in Scott Turow's book about his first year at Harvard, *One L.* He was also rumored to be the Kingsfield character in John Osborn's *The Paper Chase.* I doubt whether either of these rumors were true. Our Contracts professor would have been in his early thirties at the time of Osborn's book, slightly older in Turow's, younger than either of their characters. He was also, despite the grenade he launched at Julia, a kinder and gentler bully. Finally, the same rumors circulated about our Civil Procedure professor. Both could not be Perini/Kingsfield. I suspected that Turow and Osborn had taken liberties with a certain type of professor, a way of teaching, and their own neuroses, and created Perini/Kingsfield from whole cloth.

I understood the inclination. From the perspective of the first-year law student, sitting at an assigned seat in an amphitheatric classroom, behind rows of valedictorians and Fulbright scholars, the probing questions asked by a professor using the "Socratic method" seemed like carefully targeted missiles. The Socratic method is designed to push the student further down a slippery slope until, finally, the original position she has staked becomes untenable. (For example, a student who contends that a woman's right to choose emanates from an individual's liberty interest in her own body soon finds herself defending the proposition that the state should not regulate pornography). Even in the hands of the kindest, gentlest professor, the Socratic method, by its nature, is confrontational and intimidating.

Law students are a nervous bunch. And Harvard law students may be among the worst. Most have reached high levels of achievement by worrying as hard as they work. They worry about tests, grades, deadlines, their place in the food chain. They do not like to feel foolish. They do not like to look foolish.

But the Socratic method reduces all men to fools. There is no "right" answer. The whole point is to deconstruct, to demonstrate

how any rational position can be undermined using simple argu-
mentative modes. That, after all, is the job of the lawyer: destroy
your opponent before he destroys you. The Socratic method teaches
law students to "think like a lawyer."

When the bomb went off in the seat next to mine, in Julia's lap
I felt a giddy

Can any hand be made perfect? How to measure the value of a
perfect hand? But the professor kept at her, and several times had
the class guffawing at her expense. When it was over, I could see
beads of perspiration like a string of pearls across her forehead.

"You were great," I reassured her, and she was. This intense,
birdlike person from the heartland had battled the monster professor
and survived.

"I felt like a fool," said Julia. Her skin had flushed the same color
as her hair.

I knew she answered questions I didn't even understand. After-
ward, our classmates buzzed about how Julia had successfully par-
ried the Socratic bogeyman. Soon, students from other sections
heard the rumor, and Julia became a minor celebrity in the opening
chapter of our law school lives.

When it was time to sign up for on-campus interviews, Julia's
advice, and her brother's wisdom, weighed heavily in my decisions.
Work at the best firm that offers you a job, Julia recommended. The
experience and the name on your résumé will keep your options
open. The ACLU would always be there, anxious to hire Harvard
Law graduates, preferring those with several years' experience in
private practice, while the big law firms took you right out of law
school or not at all. "Take the money and run when you have to,"
she counseled.

We lived that summer in a writer's apartment on the Upper East Side. The living room was crammed with books, none of which we got to read as we rushed from cocktail party to dinner to theater. During the day we were the regular associates' meal ticket: lunch with us and the firm would pay. I ate at some of the finest restaurants in New York that season: Lutèce, Quilted Giraffe, Four Seasons. Partners shooed us from the office after six-thirty. And though I spent a lot of time in the library, I also attended hearings and sat in on witness interviews. We knew it couldn't last. We saw the way the permanent associates worked: the long hours, the haggard faces, the missed dates. I shared an office with a first-year associate who never left before me and never arrived after me. When his wife called, he would lower his voice to explain why he couldn't come home for dinner. I didn't feel sorry for him. Like a squirrel hoarding for the winter, I furiously collected the nuggets that were offered.

In July the lawyers and summer associates spent a day at a country club in Westchester County on a "firm outing." There was a tennis tournament, a water-polo match, lunch on the veranda, drinks by the pool, a banquet in the ballroom, dancing until midnight, chauffeured vans to shepherd us home. High-powered water pistols were distributed during dinner, capable of shooting ropes of water across a room, and the associates went to town, taking out their repressed frustrations by soaking the tuxedoed partners. The partners took their beating with good cheer; they knew we would return to the office where they would have the rest of the year to pummel the associates. It was all part of the deal, like a military academy or boot camp: to rise in the ranks you must begin as a plebe. For one day, however, the plebes had their revenge.

I was happiest then, without the burden of exams or hard work. I was being paid, essentially, to show up in a suit and be available for lunch. Of course it couldn't last; why should it? The situation was absurd: a vacation before the job began. But if anyone had asked, I would have told them I deserved it. And I believed I did.

The last two weeks of August, Julia returned to school early to work on law review, Tom went back to San Francisco, and I had the apartment to myself. I floated through the sunlit rooms, borrowed CDs playing on the stereo, the city opening before me, a new world dawning. I was being seduced, I knew, but I didn't fight it. I would have an entire year to sober up, my entire life to return the favor. I knew the routine; everyone did. I was like the man who has been taken on a t

Mary Clayton, Legal Personnel Coordinator, a copper-colored wig fastened tightly to her head, deposits a bookshelf worth of forms on the rosewood table.

"Read 'em and weep," she says.

A trickle of new associates has turned into a steady stream and soon will become a flood. Today, there are three of us in the conference room. Next Monday there will be five. In two weeks, eleven. In all, thirty-nine lawyers will join C & C this fall. In subsequent years, flusher times, the number will rise into the sixties and then seventies.

Jay Dwyer reviews the papers stacked before him. Daniel Weinstein pulls out a form and scribbles his signature. I thumb through a booklet entitled *One Hundred Years of Excellence*—a glossy pamphlet detailing the history of Crowley & Cavanaugh. Mary launches into a droning narrative about choosing a beneficiary for our life insurance policy, long-term disability, retirement planning, and other natural disasters while I secretly observe Jay and Daniel.

Jay wears an expensive suit, the fabric falling softly over his shoulders and draping his solid body like a robe. An elegant and elaborate tie nestles into the collar of his cream-colored shirt. His hair sheens as if it has been polished to his head. Two years ago he worked at C & C as a summer associate; he has returned after a clerkship with a federal appellate judge in Chicago.

Daniel looks as if he's been awake all night or slept in his suit. His red hair shoots straight up like a cartoon explosion. His tie is knotted crookedly and tilts to one side of his collar. He was at a different firm last summer, he tells me, but decided not to return after they shipped him to Pittsburgh for six weeks to review documents. It wasn't the work that bothered him, it was the lack of decent restaurants. No sane person could live without sushi.

"Any questions?" asks Mary.

I look at Daniel who looks at Jay who looks at Mary and shakes his head.

"Good," says Mary. She hands us the keys to our offices. We will occupy adjoining suites on the newly acquired twenty-eighth floor. Workmen have recently broken through the ceiling to connect a spiral staircase, a coiled thread of DNA, to the rest of the firm. We will scamper along its sugared rungs, messengers in a giant biological organism, growing, replicating, mutating.

"I love that woman," says Daniel, when we are at the elevator banks and she is safely out of earshot.

"She's harmless," Jay assures us, the voice of experience.

"Everyone's harmless when you're a summer associate," says Daniel.

"She works for you now," says Jay. "Don't let her push you around."

Who works for whom? I wonder. The firm belongs to the partners, who hire and fire. We are employees, just like Mary, serving at their whim. A bad year, a bad case, and we could be gone. No severance. Not even notice. It has happened.

"They hate the associates, personnel managers," says Daniel, as if he has taken a survey. "They all do. Snotty kids earning twice their salary."

"I don't care about her personal feelings," says Jay. "I just ask that she respect me and behave like a professional."

We step into the elevator.

Last summer Mary organized a pool party for the summer associates, an outing to Yankee Stadium, a night at the opera. She would often ring me to see if I was free for lunch with one or another lawyer. "Camp Crowley," we called C & C, and Mary was the head counselor. She called us her charges. "Aunt Mary needs to make sure you're eating properly," she would say. Now she appears to have forgotten she ever knew me.

the exam, regardless of how many years she may have practiced law elsewhere. The exam is given at a number of sites across the state, but the largest site, at the time I took it, was among the piers that jut into the Hudson River from the West Fifties. There, in a converted warehouse, several thousand hopefuls sat in endless rows, two at a table, scratching at their answer sheets while proctors prowled the cavernous alleys. Two hundred multiple-choice questions on the first day. Six essay questions on the second. More than thirty percent will fail; the rest will wonder how they passed.

I had spent two months studying for the exam: six hours a day listening to lectures on videotape, and six hours reading and memorizing "black letter" law, the rules and regulations of the legal system. While I may have learned to "think like a lawyer" at Harvard, I had few concrete thoughts. I did not know, for example, the different degrees of murder, and for how many years in prison one could be sentenced for each. I did not know when a contract had to be in writing and when it could be oral. I did not know when a bank was liable for a forged check. In short, I knew about Law but did not know the laws.

Thanks to a bar review course, in two months I crammed thousands of laws into my head. In two months I tried to learn what some law students, at schools where laws are actually taught, take three years to learn. Harvard professors shun "black letter" law, concentrating instead on theory and rhetoric. Anyone can memorize rules, they reason, but understanding the foundation for the rules, and learning how to deconstruct them, takes time. To some extent they are right; yet it's no solace for their underprepared students.

The year I took the exam, the second and final day fell on my birthday. Though my parents lived on Long Island, and I could have easily taken the train into the city, I chose to stay at a hotel three blocks from the piers. I was worried about commuting, oversleeping, accidents. Kate, my girlfriend, had offered me the futon in her studio apartment, but I had a theory about abstinence and brainpower that I didn't want to risk confirming. I also wanted to be near Julia, who was staying at the same hotel, in case I needed a last-minute mnemonic tuneup. We had promised ourselves a celebration—the passage of years and careers—on that day.

After the exam, giddy with exhaustion and relief, Julia and I tumbled into a diner off Eleventh Avenue with Tom and Kate in our wake. The place was deserted except for a short-order cook and the waitress. Julia ordered four cans of beer and carried them crooked in one arm to our table. Tom dropped a quarter in the jukebox and the song "I Fought the Law" blared through the tinny speakers.

Kate grabbed my arm and pulled me onto the black-and-white tiled floor.

"Kat," I protested, though I knew it was hopeless once she got into one of her manic moods. She was twenty-three, an editorial assistant at a publishing house, with the energy of a recent college graduate on a diet-Coke-and-deli-coffee budget.

" 'I needed money 'cause I had none,' " Kate sang as she twirled me past the booths.

I let myself spin. With each rotation I could see the faces of my friends shift like stop-action photographs. Ketchup bottles, saltshakers, milk pitchers zoomed in and out of focus. The spotted, greasy walls of the diner looked like Jackson Pollock murals.

Around and around we spun, Kate thumping time on my arm, belting out the lyrics, Julia smiling shyly, embarrassed for me, Tom laughing, encouraging Kate to twirl me faster.

When the song ended, Kate crashed against my chest. "Happy birthday," she said, her face pressed close to mine. A wet strand of hair snaked over her forehead.

The sound of a single pair of hands clapping broke the silence. The waitress ambled out from behind the counter.

"You kids must

Jackie O," says my secretary, Jackie Orlando, extending one hand. She's barely five feet tall, thin and wiry as a fishing pole, hoops of gold around her fingers, her ears, her neck. "That's what everyone calls me."

She'll be working for Jay and me, she explains. She had been assigned to a third- and a fifth-year associate, but the fifth-year left for the U.S. Attorney's office and the third-year departed to teach high school English. That's how she got us. Two lawyers to each secretary. Do I want her to answer my phone, take a letter, open my mail? Jay has already instructed her to screen his callers.

I try to imagine my need for a secretary. I type. I answer my own telephone. I don't do dictation.

She looks at me expectantly, as if a monumental task awaits to be performed. I ask her for some pencils.

"Pens, pencils, legal pads." She waves at my desk. "Yellow okay? I got two sizes. I didn't know which ones you'd like."

She marches about my office, inventorying paper clips, Post-its, sticky tabs, index cards, floppy disks, thumbtacks, steno pads, routing slips, manila folders, Redwelds, envelopes, Hi-Liters, scissors, stapler, glue. There may be something she's forgotten, but she'll remember.

"They'll give you a lesson about the phone," she says. "It's no big deal." Her fingers fly over the buttons, demonstrating speed dial, redial, conference, transfer, voice mail, intercom, night ring, privacy.

While she talks, I look out the narrow window across a small alley and into the face of another building. Hundreds of windows stare back at me. Many are filled by the bodies of men or women, dressed in suits, standing or sitting at desks piled high with paper. They gesture angrily, or pull their hair thoughtfully, or stare blankly off into space. I turn back from the window and focus on Jackie.

"They'll call you soon," she says. "You're supposed to see Caroline."

Mary told me that my first assignment would come from Caroline Strong, a senior associate working with Eric Foster. A case was going to trial. Eric had requested me specifically. Fortune was smiling.

I met Eric at the firm outing last July. Partners had been teamed with associates for the tennis tournament. Eric played tennis like a man possessed, with a ferocious serve and an unerring instinct for the ball. He took his sports, like his litigation, without prisoners. I had not played tennis in years, since I ran into a fence chasing a ball. Our combined effort led to a first-round elimination. I hope Eric has a short memory.

"When she calls," says Jackie. "You'll know."

Either Jackie is prescient or can read LED crystals from a great distance. The phone rings with a fluttering tone and Caroline's name lights up on the display.

"I can tell her you're not here," suggests Jackie.

My first day on the job; my first caller. I reach eagerly for the phone.

"Ms. Strong will see you now," says an unfamiliar voice at the other end.

I don't remember asking to see her, and I don't remember being asked. There could be a dozen senior associates clamoring for my skills. But there aren't; there's exactly one. So rather than rearranging my pencils and color-coding the Post-its, I make the ascent to Caroline's office.

*   *   *

There were 97 partners when I joined Crowley & Cavanaugh, and 205 associates. Another 20 lawyers worked in the L.A. office, and 30 more were scattered at smaller offices in Paris, London, Brussels, and Budapest. Since the early eighties, about 50 new lawyers joined the New York office each fall. Yet the partnership grew at the rate of about 1 to 3 new partners

the purgatorial role of "counsel." C & C never told an associate to leave; they were too genteel for that. Rather, like a failed suitor, the associate was expected to have the good sense to shuffle off, tail between his or her legs, to a smaller and less prestigious firm.

The process of making partner was shrouded in secrecy and myth. No one was officially nominated or notified, but everyone knew, that fateful day in the spring, when the partners met to determine the fate of the eligible candidates. After the partners emerged, the names of the lucky few would fan like brushfire through the firm, to be followed by an internal memorandum and then a public announcement on behalf of the partnership:

Crowley & Cavanaugh is pleased to announce that
Charles W. Rothman
has become a member of the firm.

Associates in their eighth year knew they had been "passed over" by the absence of their names on the memorandum. Later, they would be called into a partner's office, where their fears were confirmed or, sometimes, where they were told that the decision on their fate had been put off for another year.

Not every associate dreamed of making partner. Most denied they did. They spoke of the "experience" and the "training." They claimed they planned to take their skills to the marketplace and get another job, a better job. But tomorrow, if the head of the management committee made them an offer, they wouldn't refuse. We hadn't worked this hard, climbed our way into Harvard and then to C & C, to retreat back down the ladder with our less fortunate peers. Partnership meant not only more money, triple and quadruple our salaries, but the ability to command the lives of younger lawyers like ourselves. It meant prestige, status, a share in one of the few bastions of gentility left in the United States. Partnership at a firm like C & C, where partners were never fired, was the rare arena in American life in which one could work to attain upper-class status and then retain it permanently, with little fear of having it wrested away by an unruly board of directors or unhappy shareholders.

I never believed the lawyers who told me they weren't interested in partnership. I said the same thing, and I knew I was lying.

Caroline Strong's office is four floors above mine. I decide to walk. In the middle of each floor a staircase spirals through the landing. At each landing sits a receptionist. As I pass the receptionist on my floor, she addresses me by name. Too surprised to respond to this woman I've never met before, I simply nod. I climb four flights, and at each floor the receptionist greets me by name. I soon realize they have memorized my photo from the "Welcome Memorandum" circulated this morning, but there's a Big Brother aspect to their friendliness that spooks me.

I meander down the hushed hallways. Signed lithographs and colorful oil paintings panel the teal walls. My wingtips click over cherry floors, fall silent across Persian runners. Secretaries with headphones sit like air-traffic controllers at their aluminum bays. Their eyes flicker across computer screens, fingers flying on the keyboards. They don't look up.

After passing the same secretarial station for the third time, I decide to ask for directions. A woman in a dark blue skirt and white blouse points me toward an alcove at the end of the hall. As I approach, I can hear the raised voice of someone talking on a speakerphone and the amplified response. I stop outside the open door. A gold nameplate tells me I've arrived at the right place.

Caroline looks up and waves me into the office.

I shuffle into a room crammed with boxes and paper. The office is no bigger than mine, but it faces south onto a sunlit view of lower Manhattan. ▓▓▓▓▓▓▓▓▓▓▓▓▓▓▓▓▓▓▓▓▓▓▓▓▓▓▓▓▓▓▓▓▓▓▓▓ lobes. Her desk is cluttered with black-and-white framed photographs of her husband, the general counsel of a large corporation, and their two-year-old son. A bouquet of red roses, the only thing of color in her entire office, adorns a wooden credenza.

"Don't let him talk to you that way, Mom," Caroline says to the phone. "He walks all over you."

"He's my husband," says the voice from the speakerphone.

"I'm your daughter," says Caroline. "I don't treat you like that."

"You've got your own life."

"That's no excuse."

I signal to Caroline that I can return, and rise two inches off the seat. Caroline motions me down, raises two fingers to indicate the number of minutes remaining in the conversation.

Caroline's husband was recently featured on the cover of the *National Law Journal*. His salary was said to be $750,000 a year. He also owned, according to the article, $10 million in company stock options. Looking at Caroline now, white teeth gleaming, skin like cultured pearls, it's difficult to imagine she lacks anything.

"Kisses, dear," says the speakerphone.

"Kisses, Mom," says Caroline. She hangs up the phone and turns to me.

"I'm Caroline," she says warmly, as if we were meeting at a cocktail party. "Let me tell you what you can do for me."

*   *   *

Back in my office I reviewed the materials Caroline gave me. From what I understood, our client—Consolidated Piping—manufactured plastic piping. The city of San Diego stank of raw sewage because our client's pipes were dribbling waste into the ground, bubbling it to the surface, poisoning the water table. Thousands of miles of pipes, cracked and fetid.

The client, of course, disclaimed liability, blamed the companies that made the plastic resin, designed the system, installed the pipes. There was even an argument that San Diegoans flushed their toilets too much. All this was laid out before me in the city's "complaint" and our "motion for summary judgment."

I was not a complete neophyte. I had learned something in law school. I knew that a "complaint" is what a "plaintiff" files with the court when he commences a lawsuit. A plaintiff can be a human being or a legal entity like a corporation or the city of San Diego. The complaint lays out the relevant facts and asserts various legal theories that the plaintiff claims entitle him to relief—most often monetary damages. A "motion for summary judgment" usually occurs at a much later stage in the lawsuit, after the parties have exchanged documents and examined each other's witnesses in a process called "discovery." The summary judgment motion is usually made by the defendant and is accompanied by a "memorandum of law" in which the defendant argues that the facts that have been discovered do not entitle the plaintiff to any legal relief; therefore, the case should be dismissed. If the motion is denied by the court, the case will proceed to trial unless it is settled first.

Most cases settle. Crowley & Cavanaugh handled hundreds of lawsuits every year, yet less than a handful went to trial. This is one of the ironies of large-law-firm practice. Despite the prestige of C & C, its lawyers were woefully ignorant in the basic techniques of trial practice. While there were some partners, and even some associates, who had trial experience from stints in the Manhattan District Attorney's or U.S. Attorney's office, most C & C lawyers had never set foot in a courtroom to try a case. Fewer still had tried a case before a jury. The few who had, had learned their skills by prosecuting criminals—a very different practice from defending a civil lawsuit.

The American legal system makes a basic distinction between criminal and civil law. Criminal law involves the prosecution of crimes by the state or federal government. The prosecu~~tion~~ ~~~ prove the "guilt" of the def~~en~~d~~~

~~~~~ ~~~~ ~~~ee each ~~~ ~~~se. In civil law the question is "liability," not "guilt." Is that company liable to landowners for polluting the river? Is this corporation liable to that corporation for using a similar design for its computer software? Is my neighbor liable to me for chopping down a tree in my backyard? In each case, the plaintiff must prove liability "by a preponderance of the evidence," a far less exacting standard than "beyond a reasonable doubt." If found liable, the defendant often must pay the plaintiff money.

In the hierarchy of criminal practitioners, federal prosecutors are at the top, state prosecutors at the bottom, though there are exceptions. Certain state prosecutors' offices, such as the Manhattan District Attorney, are considered very prestigious. Among federal prosecutors' offices, certain districts—for example, the Southern District of New York, which encompasses Manhattan—are more prestigious than others.

In the civil bar, personal injury lawyers—those who handle "slip and fall" cases—are at the bottom; lawyers at large firms who represent major clients are at the top. Although, again, there are exceptions.

As in any hierarchical structure, the contours shift and mutate, subject to interpretation and re-creation. If you asked a personal injury lawyer whether he considered himself at the bottom of the civil law food chain, he would probably deny it and protest vigorously. On the other hand, his denials would have a strong whiff of defensiveness. Statistically, lawyers at large firms with corporate clients earn more than lawyers at smaller personal injury firms (though the top personal injury lawyers probably outearn everyone). Because their clients can pay more for their legal services, large law firms tend to spend more time with one case than do personal injury lawyers. This allows them to research the legal and factual issues, and file more papers with the court. Thus, these firms have developed the reputation of being more "intellectual." As a result, or maybe because of it, seventy percent of the law school graduates from Harvard, Yale, Stanford, Columbia, Chicago, and Michigan join large firms after graduation. Personal injury lawyers, on the other hand, rely on their ability to bluster and bluff insurance companies into paying their clients large awards. They are paid a percentage of the ultimate recovery; therefore, they have an incentive to handle as many cases as possible while spending the least amount of time on each. In contrast, large-firm lawyers bill by the hour. They have an incentive to work long hours on small issues.

Personal injury lawyers will tell you that lawyers at large firms don't practice law, they shuffle papers. They rarely go to court, never try cases, and examine few witnesses. They have little contact with clients or opposing counsel. The bulk of their time is spent reading books and documents. Large-firm lawyers will tell you that personal injury lawyers are "shysters," feeding off human tragedy for a living. Law, for them, is theater, lacking all intellectual rigor. The bad reputation enjoyed by the legal community, they contend, is fomented by these "ambulance chasers."

Each side is certain they could kick the other side's butt in a court of law.

Like any archetype, the ideal does not exist in its pure form. Many personal injury lawyers bill some clients by the hour, handle other cases besides "slip and fall," and even work in large group practices. Some large firms will work for a percentage fee and will also represent people who are injured. But the archetypes are important in the rhetorical struggle between plaintiff and defendant in a lawsuit, even if both sides are corporations represented by large law firms. Plaintiffs are almost inevitably characterized as "gold diggers," out for the quick buck, while defendants obfuscate, tying up truth with words and paper. The rhetoric becomes a kind of narcotic. It numbs reality and directs the mind to fantastic heights, capable of believing

heard, appealed, reversed, and denied again, the names of the lawyers like a roll call of former C & C associates. I have found the complaint, the Second, Third, and Fourth Amended complaints, and Consolidated's most recent motion for summary judgment. I am searching for earlier summary judgment motions when Barry Katz calls to invite me to lunch.

We have reservations for six at twelve-thirty, but we are four at one when finally seated. Barry has brought Madeleine Drasher, a third-year litigation associate. He has also invited Daniel, Jay, and Steven Raine, another senior associate. Steven, however, canceled at the last minute, and Jay was sent to Minneapolis to review documents in an unfolding lawsuit at a client's headquarters. Daniel tells me they didn't even give Jay time to pack, but told him to buy another suit and some shirts in Minneapolis and to bill them to the firm.

I am still grappling with this piece of information when Madeleine announces she needs to return to the office by two.

"There's always McDonald's," says Daniel.

I, too, am nervous about a prolonged absence from the office. The four feet of pleadings wait in my office like a dangerous crop. If I don't return soon, who knows what evil things will sprout?

When I was a summer associate, long lunches were a cause for celebration. I had a standing invitation from a junior associate, an

Australian lawyer working at C & C for a year. We would travel
Manhattan—he was particularly fond of Tribeca—in search of the
perfect martini. He thought nothing of disappearing for three hours
and returning with a crushing buzz. I don't know if he did any work
in the afternoon. I know I didn't.

But now as I make polite conversation while Madeleine sneaks
surreptitious peeks at her watch, I understand that most of the associates who took me to lunch last summer, with the exception of
the Australian for whom the entire year was one long summer, would
rather have been working. Two hours at lunch is two hours in which
the stack of pleadings will not get any smaller.

"So how do you like it?" Barry asks.

"It's okay," I say. "I've only got my first assignment."

"No." He laughs. "Your appetizer."

Barry is dark-haired and pale, not unlike Caroline. He looks ex-
hausted, however, with deep bruises beneath his eyes. Pallor does
not become him; it swallows him. Even his laugh lacks energy.

"Too rubbery," offers Daniel. "Hard to chew."

"Same as the work," says Barry, stretching the joke to the breaking
point.

We laugh politely, and Madeleine checks her watch.

I've been at my first real job for exactly four hours but already I
detect a subtle shift: Madeleine's curtness, Barry's quip about work.
We are not being recruited. The verb tense has changed. We've
tossed away our eligibility, traded it for a regular paycheck and a
chance at the winning number.

I eat quickly, barely tasting my food. The waiter fills and refills
my glass with bottled water. No one has ordered a drink. The three-
martini lunch is an ancient memory, if it ever existed. Today's lunch
is all diet Coke and iced tea, beverages that sparkle with aspartame
and caffeine.

After the main course, Madeleine wipes her mouth, apologizes,
and rises to leave.

"Nice to meet you," she says with an air of finality. "Good luck."

"Have a nice life," says Daniel.

He's joking, and everyone smiles, but I wonder what they really think about his wisecracks. The safest course is a low-profile, polite agreement. On the other hand, like a timid younger brother, I admire Daniel's flouting of decorum.

Julia chose carefully, with her characteristically thorough research, when she accepted a permanent offer after the summer. She knew that partners at her firm consistently earned an average of over $1 million a year, often the highest in the country. The firm also had a reputation for making a higher percentage of their associates partners; the rumor mill said if you could stick it out, they'd make you a partner. Her firm grew into a powerhouse during the takeover craze of the eighties. They specialized in nasty battles between corporations for control, utilizing a number of devices for fending off hostile takeovers, such as the "poison pill"—a strategy where a target company issues special rights to its shareholders that dilute its value if acquired by another company. Lawyers at her firm had a reputation for being aggressive, and for being Jewish.

Certain New York firms were known as Jewish firms. Julia's was one. The adjectives used to describe these firms often bordered on the anti-Semitic: "aggressive," "pushy," "hard-driving." A partner at C & C once told me, in distinguishing C & C from Julia's firm, that no one at C & C raised his voice or ran down the halls.

In truth, there were plenty of Jewish lawyers at C & C, just as there were non-Jews at Julia's firm. But C & C was known in the legal community as a "white shoe" law firm, a tag from the good old days when men were men, women were scarce, and cocktails, lunch. Julia's firm was considered nouveau riche; it had made its money in the last decades and had no roots. Again, the truth was somewhat different. All the biggest firms had made gobs of money in the eighties, and all turned to the craze for mergers and acquisitions to do it. But where Julia's firm prided itself on its takeover acumen, C & C peddled its reputation as a quiet boardroom adviser. Both firms could be ferocious, however, when it came to fighting for their clients' interests.

While many of my classmates ended up at large New York firms with a similar clientele (banks, insurers, petrochemical companies, other stalwarts of the Fortune 500), reputations differed from firm to firm. Some were reputed to be "sweatshops," others were more easygoing; some encouraged pro bono activities, taking on cases in the public interest for no fee, others were interested only in the bottom line. During the recruiting process, the firms attempted to cultivate the advantages of their perceived reputations: a firm known for hard work would tout how much responsibility its young associates received; a firm that hadn't grown as fast as its competitors would brag about its collegial atmosphere. While all large firms started new lawyers at the same salary—$85,000 at that time—the salaries did not increase at the same rate. In five years, the salaries would range from $110,000 at some firms to as much as $170,000 at firms like C & C.

A hundred seventy thousand was an absurd amount of money for a thirty-year-old to be making, but it was less than the salaries of investment bankers whose deals often led to our business, and less than the partners who gave us the work earned. Though law firms had good years and bad, since the early 1980s, C & C partners never averaged less than $600,000 a year.

Meanwhile, many lawyers, partners and associates alike, complained that they worked as hard as, if not harder than, investment bankers on the same deals and were paid a fraction of their salaries. They quickly forgot whatever had brought them to law in the first place and often jumped ship for Wall Street, where compensation was measured in seven figures. Litigators, who rarely had the same option, felt underappreciated and undercompensated. Putting a deal together was easier than picking up the pieces when it fell apart, they believed. Job security, which had once seemed inviolate and

Fluorescent lights glow in Daniel's office when I leave work at seven. Caroline ordered me not to stay late my first day, though I feel self-conscious departing before my new co-employee. But I've read the complaints and the summary judgment motions, and although three and a half more feet of pleadings await, I've covered the most important six inches. I slip out the door and click down the halogened hallways. Lights gleam in most offices. Half the secretarial stations are occupied by night staff or secretaries working overtime. Two lawyers wait at the elevator banks, each with an overstuffed briefcase. "A little light reading," one jokes.

A delivery man carrying a large plastic bag filled with Chinese food steps off the elevator as we step on. The elevator smells like fried rice and moo goo gai pan. The salty-sweet garlicky scent of New York. Lunch seems like yesterday.

I walk fast toward the subway, hunger propelling me downtown to where Kate waits at a restaurant near her apartment. Dinner, she insisted, was on her.

A cab deposits a passenger at the corner before me. She hands the driver a five-dollar bill and steps out onto the curb. A man on the opposite side of the street rushes toward the cab. The woman smiles and offers me the door. Without hesitation I accept the gift and direct the driver downtown. The man, tie flipped over his shoulder by the wind, dwindles through the rear window like a character at the end of a cartoon.

I have survived my first day of work. Not too cold; no sign of sharks. I do not know what's beyond the horizon, but I believe I can swim. I've had the lessons, studied for my exam, coated my extremities with protective balm. I'm prepared for anything.

Let them at me.

Marathon Man

I once ran the mile in 4:09.

This was BCC, before C & C, when hours were not rounded to the nearest tenth. Now, though a certain athletic prowess was touted at C & C, it was difficult to see where anyone found the time for fitness. It seemed I would have to resign myself to a slower but longer race.

A meager fitness level, however, did not stop lawyers from competing in basketball, volleyball, and softball leagues. Those who couldn't handle team sports played squash, racquetball, golf, and tennis. During the summer, the firm ran in the Corporate Challenge. C & C took these activities seriously: fistfights erupted at basketball games; middle-aged men threw out their backs to beat a play at the plate. What we lacked in the legs we made up for with our teeth. Caroline's aerobic consultant, I learned later, came to her apartment at dawn. Eric played tennis in the wee hours when the risk of heart attack was greatest. Even the softball games were scheduled when normal people were preparing for bed.

Time was a particle, composed of subatomic bits. It could be smashed and re-created in the lab. There was always more of it floating around somewhere.

Of course, C & C had its share of nonathletes who never seemed to survive to partnership. One notorious exception was a partner who weighed nearly three hundred pounds and could always be found with two cans of diet Coke in one suit pocket and a fistful of cookies in the other. I watched him one time, at a lawyers' lunch, spew crumbs in a three-foot radius as he carried on a booming conversation. It was rumored that he once came to a meeting with his dog packed inside a large lawyer's briefcase, because his wife was away for the day and had left him to care for the mutt. This lawyer was reputed to be brilliant, the favorite counsel of several major corporations; he had structured deals that no one could imagine. He was the exception who proved the rule, his grooming eccentricities tolerated by virtue of his huge billing rate and because winning, in any arena, made even the slovenly acclaimed.

At C & C a minor obsessive/compulsive disorder was practically a job requirement. There was the lawyer who lost one hundred pounds by drinking only liquids for several months. Another who kept color-coded files on every woman he dated. A third who literally ate McDonald's garbage from the bags stacked on the sidewalks. A fourth who brought a fax machine with her to the hospital delivery room. We shook our heads at such aberrations, then returned to our offices, where we refused to take notes on anything but an 8½-by-14 narrow-ruled yellow legal pad with a blue, not black, roller-ball pen. This we called normal. Thus, the same neuroses that had compelled me to run every day of the week, fifty-two weeks a year, through blizzards and smog so foul that people actually died from breathing, would become the perfect conditioning for my life as a young associate.

Day two. I stop in the hallway to say hello to another new lawyer, an anorectic young woman from Harvard. Though we were vague acquaintances in law school, we greet each other like old friends in this new landscape. Her impossibly thin wrists poke from the sleeves of her blazer like pipe cleaners with fingers. While I am a litigator, a member of the "litigation group" along with Daniel and Jay, Elizabeth is a corporate associate. She does deals; I defend the lawsuits when the deals go sour. What I know about litigation I know mostly from Julia, her brother Evan, my summer at C & C, and gossip from classmates. I am ideally suited to be a litigator, according to these sources, because I like to read, write, and speak. Litigators spend their time constr....

.... toward the meticulous, with small mouths. Thus, I am genetically fated for litigation.

Elizabeth tells me she started working at C & C on the Monday following the bar exam. She has spent the last two nights at the printer proofreading the final copy of a prospectus for a stock offering. She doesn't need sleep, she says; never has. Instead, she does an hour of yoga and meditates. She thinks she could go a week without sleep, and may actually try it just to see if she can. I think she may die.

I remember seeing Elizabeth jogging along the Charles River, her legs like brittle pencils. She jogged so slowly that elderly men would walk past her. I ask if she's still running and she tells me she's training for the New York City marathon. I wince at the damage she must be doing to her body. Isn't there a parent, a boyfriend, a friend who can shake some sense into her narrow shoulders?

"It relaxes me," she says.

In Boston I took long runs through the city's old neighborhoods, down the river, out to Newton and Brookline, into the woods behind Pine Manor College, around the track at Boston College, up the hills on Commonwealth Avenue along the marathon course. The runs were an escape from the tension of law school, the exams, the papers, the study groups, the anxiety. I ran, and the world retreated. Who am I to tell her to stop?

When I get back to my office Jackie O tells me Caroline has been looking for me.

"Where were you?" Caroline asks when I reach her on the phone.

I check my watch. It's 9:45. I was speaking with Elizabeth for fifteen minutes.

"You should always let your secretary know where you are," Caroline continues.

Jackie could see and probably hear me down the hall talking with Elizabeth. I'm about to tell Caroline that my secretary knew where I was when I realize Jackie was protecting me. Between Caroline's desire to find me and my desire to be left alone, Jackie chose me. I appreciate the confidence. On the other hand, it's a risky choice, since Caroline may have really needed me.

"She can chill for ten minutes," Jackie says after I hang up with Caroline. "She's not even a partner."

Jackie's hair is piled atop her head, a pencil thrust violently into the beehive like an afterthought or a misaimed bayonet. Her nails are blood red. Two gold hoops dangle from one ear, a hoop and a triangle from the other. She looks like a pirate.

"She's the boss," I say.

"She's not *my* boss," says Jackie. "Miss Stick-up-the-Ass from New Jersey. Miss Smarty Pants."

Caroline, Jackie, and I are all about the same chronological age. But in firm time, Caroline is a sixth-year associate, I am a mere first-year, and Jackie is my secretary. We keep no other clock.

"Pardon my French," Jackie adds.

"I don't speak it," I say. "But you should watch out, because the walls do."

I grab a yellow pad and a pen from my office. As I leave I notice that someone has stacked four boxes near the door.

"What's all this stuff?" I ask, waving at the door.

She shrugs. "Messenger brought it."

Strange packages delivered unannounced at my doorstep. The mysterious sender leaves no return address. It feels like a holiday or my birthday. I resist the urge to tear into the wrapping paper. It could be a bomb.

I ask Jackie to open the boxes. I am halfway down the hall, out of range, by the time she reaches the first one.

settlement negotiations have fallen apart. The plaintiff wants its pound of flesh. Four weeks from today, Eric will make his opening argument before the jury, the first time he has ever conducted a jury trial.

"He's trying the case," she says, as if to convince herself. "It's going to trial." After years of paper and conference calls, they will finally see a courtroom.

"*We're* going to trial," Caroline corrects herself, sweeping me onto the team with a flick of her pen. Suddenly, after one day of leisure, she's full of projects: organize the documents, prepare the experts, command the paralegals. There are one hundred thousand pieces of paper to be digested before the trial—memos, reports, correspondence. My job, and I have no choice but to accept it, is to reduce the paper to byte-sized bits in a computer database.

"How many first-years go to trial?" Caroline asks, her eyes uncreasing slightly.

"Only the ones caught insider trading."

It takes a moment for the joke to register. She looks at me through a cloud, without blinking.

"That's not funny," she says. "We had a lawyer arrested. They led him out in handcuffs."

I nod somberly; I remember the newspaper article.

"His conviction was overturned on appeal," she adds.

*   *   *

The four boxes have tripled when I return to my office. They line one end of the room, partially obstructing the window. Caroline warned that more documents were on their way. What she didn't say was that I would be buried behind them as in an Edgar Allan Poe short story.

I look at the wall of boxes with a growing panic. I'm not certain I understand Caroline's instructions and, even if I did, whether I can perform the tasks. I don't know how to organize documents into a database for trial. I don't know how to reserve a conference room or find a paralegal. None of my nineteen years of schooling have prepared me for any of these tasks.

I slump in the lumpy swivel chair behind my desk. Before me are neat rows of desk supplies. To my left, a haphazard mountain of documents. I lean backward in the chair and force myself to look straight ahead. As I do, the chair snaps, and I tumble onto the carpeting.

I lie among the ruined pieces of furniture, springs and arms and feet. The pile bristles against my cheek. A yellow stain on the ceiling, threatening to spread. Voices in the hallway like atonal music. Jackie's face.

"Hello?" she says.

I rise from the wreckage and brush my aching hip.

"It collapsed," I explain.

Jackie sorts through the nuts and bolts while I call Mary Clayton. Though someone else is responsible for office furniture, all roads eventually lead to Mary. I tell her Caroline needs a conference room and three paralegals, and I need a new chair.

"What happened to your chair?" she asks suspiciously.

"Ex-chair," I correct her, in my best Monty Python accent.

I imagine her pinched lemon lips and tight wig. She shakes her head disapprovingly.

"Excuse me?"

"My ex-chair, former chair, lost but not forgotten chair," I continue, the joke already grating on me.

Mary does not appreciate my comedy routine. "We'll have to or-der a new one," she clucks. "These things take time." Then she hangs up.

I stare mournfully at the receiver, the steady crackle of static like the buzz of an angry insect. "She hates me," I say to Jackie

nearly as tall as Julia, but more substantial, the former co-captain of Princeton's women's squash team.

Abby takes charge, a role cemented during the last year of working together on this case. Howie's the prankster. Wilson, detailed and thorough. Abby suggests we group each document into one of fifteen categories. Wilson will enter them into a database on a laptop com-puter from which they can be identified if they are needed at trial. "We can revise as we go through them," she says to me.

"You know the documents," I say, hoping to appear reasonable rather than dim-witted. In fact, no one knows these documents. The lawyer who selected the papers to be produced and copied, and his criteria for selection, have faded from C & C's collective memory. At best, the paralegals know the small slice of documents that have been identified as relevant by the lawyers working on the case.

"I can't remember every category," Howie moans.

Abby flips a switch near the lights in the conference room and the wall slides away to white board. She picks up a thick marker and writes out the categories. The marker squeaks as she loops through the letters.

"Anything else?" she asks.

We shake our heads, scratch our noses, rub our feet against the floor.

The rosewood conference table fills with paper. Wilson's fingers click over the keys. Soda cans assemble in front of Howie as he slowly catalogs documents. He huffs and shuffles and shifts in his seat.

The room is stuffy and smells of old toner. Abby opens the door. The nosy and inquisitive poke their heads into our business, ask how the war is going, inquire after our commander. Abby shuts the door.

Each piece of paper is a mystery to me. I examine it from every side. A letter from the manufacturer of plastic resin to our client complaining about late payment. A memo from the quality control department to the purchasing department detailing the presence of "nonconforming materials" in the latest batch of resin. A pamphlet touting the benefits of PVC piping for sewage facilities. I read them slowly, fixating on the personalities behind the documents. Did J. Arnez withhold delivery until he got paid? What will B. Smith do with fifty cubic feet of spoiled resin? Who are these smiling workers pictured in the sewage treatment plant?

The papers fly from Abby's hands and into a box marked "reviewed." I read the entire pamphlet on sewage treatment before I remember why I'm reading it. When I finish, I have to go back and review the whole document before I can catalog it.

"This isn't extrusion," says Wilson, holding up a page I've marked with a red "4" on a Post-it.

I look at a purchase order that has nothing to do with the process of turning resin into piping. "Thanks for catching that," I say as casually as I can.

Thousands of pieces of paper, each with a story to tell, each forgotten until the eve of trial. I do not know anything about how the documents were gathered, but I know they are here now, waiting to be identified so that Eric will have instant access to the fine points of extrusion. He passed his order to Caroline, who interpreted it for me, who called for paralegal assistance.

Two thoughts occur to me as I flip through the pages. Why have three years passed before anyone attempted to catalog the documents? And, after three years, when all the witnesses have been examined and all relevant documents identified, what possible use could be made of the thousands of unidentified documents? The questions are interrelated: if the documents were not important enough to be cataloged, why must they be cataloged now; if they are important, isn't it too late to do this? I don't ask these questions because I'm sure there's an answer; there's some reason why I am sitting in this conference ~~~

...~~~ to crack. He will confess that while laying sewer piping, trucks dumped giant boulders on the pipes, splitting them hopelessly despite their phenomenal tactile strength and quality control. Thanks to you and your document database, Eric will say, victory was snatched from the jaws of plaintiff's lawyers.

Slowly I push that rock up the hill. Slowly it will tumble back down.

As the hour approaches seven, my stomach wakes me from my slumbers. I regard the squad of paralegals warily. We have been working for nearly five hours, slowly cataloging our way through the documents, and the piles don't look any smaller. I wonder what Kate is doing; I promised I would call. I consider announcing that we will return tomorrow. I am the lawyer, after all. I am in charge. But they are working furiously, oblivious to my biological and domestic needs. If I tell them to call it a day, they might revolt, scoff at my idleness, lampoon my absent backbone, report me to the partners. With every passing minute their hourly wage increases; mine diminishes. They are paid overtime.

Finally, Abby asks if we want to order dinner. Howie agrees enthusiastically. Wilson asks me how late we're going to work.

"We've got a ton of documents," I muse noncommittally.

"And not a lot of time," adds Abby.

"You guys don't have to stay," I offer magnanimously, hoping they will leave so I can call Kate.

Halfhearted murmurs of protest bubble from their mouths. Of course they'll stay; now that I've offered, to leave would be certain death.

"Chinese," says Howie.

"It's always Chinese," says Abby.

"We're not doing Indian. Last time I was on the can all night."

"Thank you for sharing," says Abby. She turns to me. "What do you want?"

"Chinese sounds fine," I say, resigning myself to a Kateless night.

Howie produces an accordion file of menus: Chinese, Japanese, Indian, Mexican, Italian, Russian, French, Northern Californian, Southern Californian, Southwestern. Obviously, this is an old routine for him. The protocol of ordering, however, eludes me. I have been taken to dinner by C & C, but I have never eaten dinner at C & C. As a summer associate, the latest I ever stayed was eight o'clock, and only twice. Most nights I left by 6:30. How much should I spend? Who pays? How do they pay? I am a late-night neophyte.

"Shun Lee is the best," says Howie, pushing an expensive menu in front of me.

"Can we afford this?" I ask.

"We've been eating there all summer."

"You've been eating there," Abby corrects him.

Howie reassures me that the client never sees the bill. At the end of the month it receives one statement that buries meals in a single line with transportation and travel. No one asks to see restaurant receipts.

"They're making you stay," he adds. "They *should* pay."

At college track meets our coach would give us four dollars for dinner. The choice was always McDonald's or Burger King. And that felt like a luxury. *They gave us money for dinner.* A Big Mac and fries was all it took to make me happy.

I write orders on a manila envelope. Howie, Abby, and Wilson know the menu by heart. I scrutinize it carefully before choosing steamed dumplings and spicy chicken with sesame seeds. The bill comes to $120. Howie asks for my credit card, which I give him because Abby and Wilson do not balk, and he phones in the order.

In what hardly seems enough time to walk to the restaurant, let alone prepare a meal, the food arrives. First, a security guard calls

cardboard boxes. We sort through the dishes, shuffling them like pucks across the table. Wilson spills a sack of plastic cutlery that clatters onto the rosewood. Howie distributes diet Cokes. When all is arranged, we dive into the food, a glorious moment of silence while we take our first bites.

I have an oddly satisfied feeling as I look around the conference room at the bowed heads of the paralegals, *my* paralegals. The late hour, the warm smell of Chinese food, our common goal. The room seems positively cozy, and I feel my chest swell with appreciation for their presence.

We have an almost impossible number of pages to conquer, 87,502, according to the numbers the paralegals have stamped in sequential order on each document with the "Bates stamper." Nearly 22,000 pages per person. But nothing seems impossible when we work together. We can rise to any challenge, and we will.

I stare intently into my dumplings. I have always cried at sentimental movies, the death of pets, string quartets. I do not want to add document databases to the list.

Daniel is still at his desk, his desk lamp glowing and a stack of casebooks open before him, when I return for my suit jacket and briefcase.

"Going home tonight?" I ask as I swing by his open door.

He looks up, distracted. "What time is it?"

It's nearly midnight. The firm hums like a submarine with a skeleton crew. I have reviewed nearly two thousand pages today, reading some, scanning others, grateful for the two hundred page documents that can be cataloged with a quick glance at their titles.

At the end of the hallway a cleaning person emerges from an office, shuts the lights, and closes the door. Her cart rolls across the cherry floors, wheels racketing, then rumbling, as she bumps up onto the carpets.

"It's late," I tell him.

Daniel's tie is a loose knot drooping around his neck, a noose ready to hang, the top two buttons of his shirt undone. His explosive hair leans dangerously to one side of his head, a blaze ready to ignite. The computer monitor casts an otherworldly pallor across his cheeks.

"I've got a few cases to Shepardize," he says as he scrolls through a search of case citations.

A litigator's work is never done. At any moment a court could reverse, challenge, question, vacate, distinguish, follow, or explain a previous ruling. In Hawaii, the Ninth Circuit, it is only four o'clock.

I grab my jacket off the hook behind my door. "Don't stay too long," I say, giddy with a late-night buzz. "Tomorrow's a school day."

He huffs mightily, his nostrils flaring like flags. He doesn't think I'm funny.

Outside, the avenues glitter like galaxies. A crisp breeze, the end of summer, snaps at my jacket vent. A cruising cab slows, honks, but I wave him on. It's too late to visit Kate; too early to go home alone. I walk north, toward the park. I can almost smell the trees. The sidewalks are empty, flat, and wide as a midwestern prairie. No life stirs. At the corner, a man in a cardboard box asks me for a quarter. I fish through my pockets and give him all my change. He disappears back into his crate like a Beckett creation.

Streetlights blink from green to yellow to red, illuminating the concrete surfaces in a crayoned quilt. I take one step off the curb. My back to the wind. If I opened my arms, I could almost fly.

Another cab slows and honks, and this time I give in. I climb inside and shut the door. Drive, driver, I command. Giddy-up.

"They will," Abby says. "The day before trial."

"That's too late for us," says Howie.

"It'd be worse if we went to trial."

"Living in San Diego for three months doesn't sound so bad."

"You'd never see San Diego. You'd be in a hotel room or a courthouse."

I don't tell them that if anyone goes to San Diego it will be Wilson, Caroline's favorite. Yesterday Caroline warned that I probably wouldn't go either. "Someone has to man the fort," she said. She meant that I'd stay behind in the library, researching issues that they phoned in to me from the courthouse.

"Is there any more food?" asks Howie, eyeing Abby's container.

Abby shuffles it to him.

"These late nights make me hungry," Howie says.

"It's only two in the afternoon."

"I know, but night is coming."

We've been here since nine. Abby was first; she opened the conference room and turned on all the lights. Her blond hair, usually pulled back in a tight ponytail, or twisted around her head in some fancy braid, spills freely over her shoulders. Howie hasn't shaved. Everyone wears jeans. Although we were the first people on the thirtieth floor, by noon about a third of the office lights were lit, and a small crew of overtime and weekend secretaries buzzed about the floor.

I push my soggy plate into the trash and return to the papers on my side of the table. As I review them, trying to decide what categories they belong to, I can't conceive of their relevance. I've been doing this for nearly a week, and I don't know anything about practicing law yet, but I know that no one is going to enter ten thousand invoices into evidence at trial. There's no dispute over how much piping was sold or to whom. Still, I mark each invoice in its appropriate category and Wilson dutifully enters it into the computer.

I find myself thinking once more about the lawyer who collected the documents. How did he find them, where did he go, what did he do? Boxes and boxes of papers, gathered by an attorney already forgotten, in a process no one could reconstruct. No trace remains except his invisible fingerprints, the ghostly memory of his billable hours on every page.

Again I wonder whether I'm wasting my time, and the client's money, sitting in the conference room cataloging invoices. I imagine Eric popping up in the middle of trial, checking an invoice on his laptop computer. "Just a minute, sir," he would say, "do you mean to tell this court that invoice number 2-B00345X78 authorized the shipment of ten tons of A1 resin? I happen to have a copy of that invoice right here. Please take a close look at it." The courtroom hums and buzzes. The witness stammers. The judge pounds his gavel on the podium. Order in the court!

But Caroline gave me this assignment. She told me to input every document in a database. She did not tell me to use my discretion. When I meekly questioned whether there might be some papers we could omit, she looked at me as if deciding whether I was this year's troublemaker. "Eric wants all the documents in a database," she repeated. Did there need to be another reason?

Now as I pick up speed, I deliberately overlook some documents. Obvious ones, like invoices and brochures, that I'm certain won't be needed for trial. I leave them in their file folders, as if they have been returned there by Wilson or Howie after being entered in the computer. No one will review my work, I reassure myself; there isn't enough time. My secret omissions will go unchecked, blindly back to the files where the documents will cease to exist. They couldn't be found even if Eric really wanted to read every invoice, which he

And if they don't? I'll blame the paralegals.

Monday morning. Daniel's door is open and his desk lamp on, but the overhead lights are out and he's nowhere to be seen. Jay is back at his desk reading the *The Wall Street Journal* after a week in Minneapolis. He offers me a section.

I sit on a small chair in his office and scan the paper. As far as I can tell, the war in the Middle East is driving the price of treasury bonds upward. Elsewhere, the death of an Asian leader has caused his country's currency to plummet in value. If Moscow were burning, it would be reported under "Other News."

"Is there a sports section?" I joke.

Jay looks at me sourly. "Read the *Post*," he says.

On the walls he has already hung his Yale diploma along with a signed photograph of his judge and his three bar admissions: New York State, and the Southern and Eastern districts of New York. This, and our five minutes of conversation on the first day of work, is all I know about him. His college diploma is conspicuously absent.

"Did you go to college?" I ask.

He regards me warily.

"I thought you might have been one of those geniuses who skip college and go right to law school," I explain.

"Villanova," he says to the newspaper. "It's being framed."

I wait for him to explain, because I know an explanation will follow.

He looks up. "Track scholarship," he says.

Jay is five ten, about 180 pounds, without an ounce of muscle on his body. Villanova, I know, has one of the best track teams in the country. I can't imagine in what event Jay could win a scholarship.

"Eight hundred meters," he says. "I quit after my freshman year."

I ran the eight hundred, the metric equivalent of the half mile. It's possible Jay ran, but he doesn't look like any eight-hundred-meter runner I've ever seen.

"What's your PR?" I ask.

"One fifty-seven," he says. "In high school."

A decent time for a high school runner, but I doubt Villanova would have offered him a scholarship when they had their pick of runners from all over the world. He may be lying, but I don't know him well enough to call his bluff.

"I used to run," I say, to test him.

A small chink of sunlight stabs through the window, illuminating a patch of bare wall.

"Good for you," he says. Then he turns back to the paper, leaving me to ponder whether the rise in unemployment will lead to a reduction of interest rates, and whether there will be jobs for lawyers after the Fall.

At about eleven, Daniel wanders into the office.

I am wearing an olive-green suit and a flowery tie despite summer's last gasp. Daniel grimaces at my fashion faux pas as he passes me in the hallway by the secretarial stations. "Going to the beach?" he asks. He wears a gray suit and a striped tie, a safe and season-proof choice. He slouches into his office and turns on the computer. Jay is typing away at his. Though we three are litigation associates, Daniel has been given a research and writing assignment, and Jay has already traveled to meet a client, which seem more significant than my quasi-clerical task. They, on the other hand, covet my imminent trial experience; Daniel told me I "lucked out." I'm not sure that sitting in a conference room qualifies as trial experience, but I haven't dashed their misconceptions.

Jackie announces she going downstairs to the lobby café coffee; do I w...

...David, a female ...announced.

"Hello? Anybody home?" says Jackie.

"Milk, no sugar," I say meekly.

I retreat to my office and into my cobbled-together chair, careful to avoid leaning backward. My back hurts. My skin feels like tofu. Five months ago I was running sixty miles a week; now I can barely walk home from the subway.

I stare into the documents that I've retrieved from the conference room. After seven straight days in the same room, including the entire weekend, I've granted myself a change of venue. When I look up, Mary, coral face and penny-colored wig, stands at my door.

"Can I come in?" she says as she comes in.

She deposits herself in the seat across from my desk and regards me with a mixture of disdain and contempt.

"You broke your chair," she says.

"I didn't," I protest. "It was broken."

"You broke it," she repeats. "And now we'll have to find you another."

She spreads open an office furniture catalog. Suddenly, I am greedy at the prospect of new furniture. I want bookshelves and an end table and a halogen lamp. I want an ergonomically designed armchair with headrest, swivel legs, and back support. I want—a sofa!

"These are the colors," says Mary, pointing to puke green, insipid blue, and shit brown. "These are the styles."

"What about this one?" I ask, pointing to a black leather swivel chair with gleaming titanium legs.

Mary frowns. "There are two styles and three colors."

"I'll find my own chair," I suggest brightly. "The firm can reimburse me."

"These are the chairs," Mary repeats.

"The partners have their own chairs."

"When you're a partner, you can choose your chair."

"I'll pay for the chair," I offer helpfully.

Mary squints at me; her boar eyes darken. "Do you want a new chair?"

"I do," I say.

"Blue, green, or brown?" She taps the glossy catalog page.

"Blue," I sigh.

Mary closes the catalog with a firm snap that resonates with victory. "Eight to twelve weeks," she says.

It's useless to protest, I know. The partners love Mary; they think she does a great job. Without Mary, one partner told me last summer, there would be no buffer between lawyers and the cold, cruel world. Now I think he meant that without Mary, there would be no buffer between the partners and disgruntled associates. Instead of admitting to a furniture hierarchy, the partners can shift the burden to Mary. They can work while Mary gladly plays the Grinch.

I'm about to complain anyway when Jackie arrives with my coffee. Mary squints at the cup and then at me, as if confirming her darkest thoughts about associates.

"Coffee," says Jackie brightly, her hoop earrings jangling like wind chimes.

"How nice for you," says Mary as she packs up the catalog and leaves the office.

"Raid," says Jackie when Mary has gone, "would kill that bug up her ass."

* * *

After my second week of cataloging documents, I was enlisted to help Eric prepare our experts. Eric instructed Caroline to instruct me on possible areas for cross-examination. I had talked to Eric twice since my arrival at C & C, once accidentally in the elevator, and a second time when he was on the speakerphone in Caroline's

elevator he kept them averted, as if afraid of what sinister secrets might be revealed. He was dark-haired, though not as dark as Caroline, and permanently sunburned, his skin toasted too many times on the tennis court.

I had no clue how to prepare an expert or what areas of cross-examination they might encounter. Who were our experts? What did they do? What would they say?

It's difficult to imagine the terror a young associate feels when she is given a new assignment. Most of what she learned in law school involved legal research and writing. She is well suited to preparing a memorandum on when damages should lie for interlocutory intervention under rule 65(c). She can go to the library, look up the annotated Federal Rules of Civil Procedure, read the paragraph summaries of cases following the rule, find the ones relating to damages, pull the volumes from where they are located on the shelves, read the cases, compile them, analogize and construct a legal argument.

But eventually every associate must venture into dangerous and strange new territory. It is one thing to research a principle of law—when do damages lie under rule 65(c)?—quite another matter to apply specific facts to that principle. Let's say you researched the law and found that you can get damages for interlocutory interventions but only in certain situations: when your adversary acted *wrongfully*. Well, what does *wrongfully* mean? You read the cases and find some definitions for *wrongfully*, but they're vague and broad. What you really have discovered are specific factual situations in which a court decided a party's actions were wrongful. Are those situations like yours? How should you know? You don't know anything about the facts of your case.

This is the first moment of panic. You think you should know. Maybe you missed something when you were given the assignment. Did you listen closely enough? You squirm and twist in the library seat. Finally, you straighten your backbone and return to the office of the senior associate who gave you the assignment. He's very busy, but he takes two seconds to explain the facts of an extremely complicated matter to you. You nod, but now you're really in a panic. He's filled your head with all manner of minutiae, most of which you don't understand, none of which help, all of which only complicate the inquiry. This is when panic mutates into hysteria: the more you learn about a case, the more you need to know.

Every associate deals with mounting hysteria differently. Some pore over the facts in great detail, learning everything they can about the case and charging the client an enormous sum of money in their efforts to grip an expanding universe. Others, like me, throw their hands up in despair, go back to their offices, and write the memorandum with the limited knowledge they have, emphasizing the facts from other cases, minimizing the facts from their own case, hoping no one will expose their ignorance. Most of the time it works, because no one reads the memorandum.

Learning the facts of a case is the most important part of practicing law and, of course, not taught in traditional law school classes. No professor dumps one hundred thousand pages of documents on a student's desk and tells him to figure out what's going on. No one introduces the student to fifty corporate employees and asks her to interview them in order to understand the issues. The facts of a case, when they are presented, are summarized in neat paragraphs, easily digested, simplified. Who can blame the first-year associate for panicking? She's never seen a fact in the wild before.

Thus my problem in preparing the experts. I didn't know the detailed facts of our case. I wrote one question: *Why do you think the pipes leaked?* Then, I revised the question: *What is your expert opinion as to why the pipes leaked?* Then I remembered I was supposed to be preparing the experts for cross-examination, when they will be examined by lawyers for the

to finish the documents and prepare questions for the experts.

It was going to be a long week.

We work through our third weekend. Three paralegals and one associate. Combined, we bill the client $500 per hour, not including meals, transportation, and secretarial overtime. Abby and Howie snipe at each other. Wilson bleaches into the computer screen. I slump at the opposite end of the long conference table, scratching expert questions on a yellow legal pad with my pencil.

Eventually, I had returned to Caroline to ask for guidance. She, too, seemed near meltdown, sallow rather than pale. There were last-minute motions to file: attempts to restrict the scope of evidence introduced at trial, to strike certain testimony, prohibit opinions from being offered. She regarded me sympathetically, perhaps seeing her own panic reflected on my face. Then she told me to start with the "depositions," the pretrial examinations of the witnesses, in which the experts were asked the bases for their opinions. The deposition transcripts of the experts, ours and theirs, constituted nearly two thousand pages.

Now, as I read through the transcripts, I am presented with a premade outline of questions our experts have already been asked by lawyers for the plaintiff as well as testimony from plaintiff's experts who disagree with the opinions of our experts. It's a lively debate involving polymers and organic chemistry, and reminds me of why I dropped my premed classes in college.

"I'm dying," Howie moans.

"Can you make him shut up?" Abby asks me.

I'm in charge here, I remember. I can't have the paralegals killing each other. It would be hard to bill the client for the funerals.

"We're almost done," I say. I see Wilson raise an eyebrow from behind his laptop computer and realize I have no idea whether we are. I'm happy to have graduated to expert preparation, however, and to leave the minutiae of document databasing to the paralegals. It makes me feel more like a lawyer, even though for two weeks the only difference between our work was that I billed the client nearly twice as much per hour and they knew what they were doing.

"I'm never going to law school," says Howie.

"You don't do this in law school," I reassure him.

"You have to wait until you graduate?" he asks incredulously.

"You don't become a partner overnight." I sound like someone's mother, I think.

"What's so great about making partner?" Howie asks. "You think Eric is happy?"

"He's not stuck here with you," says Abby.

"He's stuck upstairs with Caroline."

"Actually," I say, "they're at Caroline's apartment." Caroline and her husband live on Fifth Avenue, in an apartment rumored to be as large as a suburban house. She told me she and Eric would be working there this weekend, preparing for trial, if I needed to reach her.

"See, that's one advantage of being a partner," says Abby. "You get to work at home."

"Caroline's not a partner."

"She might as well be."

I raise both hands, asking for a minute of peace. I've read two hundred pages of the first of seven deposition transcripts. I'd love to argue with Howie all day about the costs and benefits of a legal education, the diminishing levels of personal satisfaction in my chosen profession, the limited opportunities for equity participation in large-firm practice, but I've got plenty of other ways to pass the time.

These paralegals are earning about $28,000 a year. With overtime, they can make $50,000. When they work late, their dinners and cab fare are paid for. Th

I don't want to suffer," he says. "Especially for a guy named Art."

Monday morning, bleary-eyed, I stumble past Jay's office. His feet are propped on his desk, *Wall Street Journal* open, a white collar on a blue shirt framing his neatly groomed face.

"How's the running?" he asks as I pass.

I stop by his door, then poke my head inside. I tell him I worked all weekend; I haven't had a chance to go outside, let alone exercise.

"Marathon's coming," he says, as if it were a tornado or a tsunami.

"I don't run marathons," I remind him, though a scholarship athlete should know the difference between a middle-distance and a distance runner.

"Not you," he says. "Me. I do it every year."

I can almost believe that once upon a time he ran a half-mile. But the marathon? Is he testing me? Is he joking? I look carefully at his Yale diploma, as carefully as I can while pretending to listen to him. It appears real, his name inked in the proper place. The photograph from his judge looks real, too, with a real signature, though it could be anyone's; I've never seen his judge's handwriting.

"You can run with Elizabeth," I say. It would be a close race, I think.

"She looks like she could use the help."

"Are you offering?"

"Not if I have a choice."

In high school I knew a kid who, in college, claimed to be best friends with the son of a famous politician. It turned out this kid was a pathological liar and didn't even know the politician's son. But later on he did, in fact, become close friends with the politician's son, which made him either a very successful, or very unsuccessful, liar.

I don't want to learn which type Jay is. Instead, I retreat to my office behind the excuse of the documents.

I collapse in the stiff-backed chair I stole from a conference room when my repair job became too wobbly to trust. My family waves to me from a photograph. On the other side of my desk, a black-and-white Kate blows a winking kiss. The walls are still bare. My desk empty of papers except for a newly printed version of cross-examination questions for our experts. After I went home at three in the morning, I left my penciled scrawlings with the word-processing department. Now, a new day, a new document. Nice font, good margins, excellent print quality; as long as I don't read it, it looks professional.

I decide to take the list of questions to Caroline's office myself. I haven't adjusted to the messengers who canvass the floors, picking up papers from one office, delivering them to another. Lawyers don't even need to move, just shuffle documents from In box to Out box, where they will be transported by secretary to messenger to the office down the hall.

I wait for the elevator, avoiding the forced cheer of the receptionists. When the elevator arrives, it is crowded with lawyers arriving late, two messengers, and a woman pushing a cart loaded with expensive breakfast pastries and several thermoses of coffee. I squeeze inside, up against the cart. Sugar dusts my suit jacket. At the next floor, the woman departs but before she does, one of the lawyers grabs a Danish. "We're paying for it," he jokes to his companion, though a client probably is.

Caroline's floor seems busier and more expensively appointed and lighted than mine. Most of the offices belong to partners or senior associates, while my floor is a labyrinthine warren of cubbyholes. The wood here is darker and richer, the paintings by brighter stars of the modernist era, the aluminum more highly burnished. None of the secretaries resemble Jackie or the younger women who tend to junior associates. Here, th

"You look like shit," she says when she hangs up the phone.

"I was here all weekend."

She straightens; an ebony strand of hair falls over one eye. "You know Consolidated settled?"

"Settled?"

"Friday."

"Friday?"

She squints at me. "You didn't work all weekend on the trial?" she says.

I lower my head like a cow in the wind. The gusts off the prairie sting my battered face and hands.

"The paralegals, too?"

I nod.

"We'll have to write off their hours," she says petulantly, as if she'll have to give the time back to the technicians to refashion in the lab.

"We didn't know," I protest.

"Someone should have told you," she says.

Someone, I wonder, who?

At six-thirty that evening I close the door and take off my clothes. For a moment I stand stark naked in the middle of the office, poised on the brink of anything, like that moment in a car on a highway when a slight swerve will change everything forever. Then I quickly slip on shorts, a T-shirt, and running shoes, purchased that afternoon, and leave my suit hanging on the back of the door. I'll carry it home another day. For now, I'm free of it.

Daniel is still at his desk, Jay at his, as I sneak past their offices. They don't see me. The elevator banks are empty; the C & C rush hour is at least an hour away.

My first case has resolved itself in an unsatisfying fashion. Not with a bang, but with a whimper. The city of San Diego has been cowed into accepting a meager $5 million from fear of our massive document database and smartly prepared experts. My work was not in vain. My time well spent. I can sleep peacefully knowing that, if called upon, I would have kicked butt.

Outside, on the street, the buildings of Park Avenue rise gray and tall like patrician forebears. I take a tentative step along the sidewalk. One foot, then the other, and I am moving. The sun still shines weakly; there is even a tree.

I quicken my stride. Pedestrians scatter like pigeons. Soon, I am flying across the pavement, my feet barely touching ground. I check my stride in the glass façades. A mild compulsive disorder can be a beautiful thing.

I look great.

The Vertical Rule

I was a free man, and for several weeks I literally had nothing to do. I read every piece of mail that came across my desk: advertisements for Practicing Law Institute classes, the *Securities Law Reporter,* advance sheets reporting Supreme Court cases, the *New York Law Journal,* the American Bar Association newsletter. I did some computer research and found articles on Law and Literature, an academic subject that interested me. I printed the articles and read them leisurely, with my feet propped on my desk.

I had fallen into the cracks at C & C, somewhere between the settlement of Consolidated and the assignment of a new matter. I considered telling Caroline I had no work, but I worried she would wonder why I didn't tell anyone earlier, or she would give me something awful to work on. There was a partner in charge of reviewing the time records of associates and assigning them new cases when their time slipped below acceptable levels, although work often came from more informal routes. I kept silent, figuring that the assignment machinery would function properly and he would give me another case. In the interim I charged my time to "Legal Education," an amorphous category that I hoped covered what I was doing.

Crowley & Cavanaugh lawyers lived (and died) by the billable hour. I had calculated that if I billed at least eight hours every day, not including weekends and vacation, by the end of the year I would have nearly two thousand hours. Two thousand seemed like the magic number; it was the minimum most associates said the firm expected. Of course, plenty of lawyers billed more than two thousand hours, and some billed less, but two thousand would not trigger any alarm bells.

Billing eight hours a day, however, did not mean working nine to five. Not every minute at work is a billable minute. Lawyers eat lunch, they talk to each other, they talk to friends, they go to the bathroom, they stare into space, they read legal publications that are not related to a particular client—none of these activities are billable: you can't charge a client for staring into space. Over the years, I was surprised how many times I added my hours up at the end of a long day and they did not total eight.

I kept the billable bits of the day on scraps of paper and Post-its that hung like flags from my telephone: *4.8 hrs.—review depos.; 2.5—cat. docs. for datab.; 3.0—prep. expert x-examine.* The minutes accounted for like neat stacks of coins. At the end of the week I transferred my scrawlings (if I could read them) to a form that Jackie entered into the computer. One advantage of having no work was the simple number I wrote every day: *8.0—Legal Ed.*

Kate didn't think I should complain about my newfound leisure. "That's why they invented television," she said.

Her studio apartment was crowded with manuscripts, dogeared, red-penciled tomes as hefty as doctoral dissertations. She read them in bed, after dinner, or on the couch, before dinner arrived, or during dinner. When I noted that she was working harder than I, she promised that big-firm math would eventually catch up to me.

She was right. A first-year associate, who billed at $150 an hour, multiplied by 2,000 hours, minus his salary of $85,000, cleared $215,000 for the partners, less overhead. Every extra hour that the associate worked, once the firm had covered its expenses, went directly into the partners' pockets. Each year, as the associate's billing rate increased, so did the partners' take. Like a giant Ponzi scheme, profits depended on an unending source of associates entering at the bottom of the pyramid, funneling cash up the chain, and departing before making partner. The greater the ratio of associates to partners, the greater the profits. No one forgot the simple equations. That was why the partners told us to bill clients for the time we spent thinking

roast beef sandwiches, three brownies, and a carton of chocolate milk. Lunch is free. Next door, on the unwindowed side of the building, the support staff dines. Until this year, their lunch was not free; but recent decisions of the IRS requiring equal treatment of employee benefits, upheld by the tax court, have imposed freedom upon them, to the chagrin of C & C partners.

Daniel takes an enormous bite of his sandwich while I politely turn away and watch our colleagues gathering provisions like hibernating animals. The days grow shorter, the nights are long; we hoard to survive. At night, when he's working late, an associate on my floor slips a CD into an enormous boom box in his office. "*What* is he listening to?" Jay complains. "That's not music," I agree, solemnly mimicking my parents, "it's noise."

"So what are you working on?" I ask Daniel, to say anything, jump-start a conversation, the awkward stillness hanging between us like damp weather. I realize that this is the brilliance of the free lunch: the typical conversation opener is always "What are you working on?" Lunch may be free for C & C attorneys, but it's not free for C & C's clients.

He tells me he's drafting a section of a brief, an argument that a public utility cannot be liable for misrepresentations about its filed rates, even if the misrepresentations are deliberate and fraudulent.

Daniel seems to be one step ahead of me on the law firm learning curve. When I was cataloging documents, he was writing research memoranda. Now he's graduated from memoranda and moved on to briefs. "How can that be?" I ask.

"Customers are presumed to know the provisions of a filed tariff," he says. "Public policy favors uniform application of rates."

I have no idea what he is talking about, or why it should matter, but I nod as if I do.

"What's their best argument?" he asks.

I know he's merely proving the virtue of C & C's not-really-free lunch policy, but I don't want to talk about his research or his argument, and I certainly don't want to be subjected to a round of the Socratic method.

I am saved from answering by Barry Katz, who appears at our table with a green salad and a cup of coffee. He looks like he desperately needs both. "You guys leaving?" he asks.

I tell him we'll stay. He seems relieved. I think that we never really leave the awkward social experience of the high school lunchroom behind. We're always searching for a friendly table.

"How you guys doing?" he asks me. "You working on anything?"

"Research," I answer vaguely.

He nods; he's barely listening. "When you're done," he says, "I've got an interesting project if you've got the time."

I can use the work, and the hours, though his specialty—rein-surance litigation—sounds as boring as televised dentistry. I know it's not his fault; in fact, I like Barry—his droopy eyes, his shuffling nervousness—but his interesting threshold appears to be extremely low.

"Sure," I say. "As long as it's interesting."

"Oh, it is," says Barry.

"Yeah," says Daniel, "that's what they all say."

Barry's "interesting" project turned out to be a compendium of all cases that had addressed the issue of "alter ego" liability for a corporation. The client of the partner for whom Barry worked wanted to know the factual situations in which courts had "pierced the corporate veil," i.e., found a parent corporation liable for the acts of its subsidiary. Normally, courts respect the separate corporate identity of companies even if one company is entirely owned by another. However, in certain circumstances, usually involving fraud or where the company itself ignores the corporate formalities, a court will

sociates, reading the federal and state digests from other jurisdictions. When I found a relevant case, I would write a brief summary of the facts and the legal holding. Soon my memorandum had expanded to twenty pages. But when I returned to Barry, he asked whether I was certain I had found all the cases. "Not *all* of them," I said. The horror must have been visible on my face, because Barry commiserated. "Stanley is the Great Dictator," he said about the partner for whom he worked, blaming him for the scope of the project. I wondered, however, who was really the dictator. I saw the way Barry treated his secretary, as if she had a third-grade education. Once I heard him call her a "dope," another time a "clod." To me he was always polite, but clearly he harbored a frustrated despot. Was it Stanley's influence or his own impotence, or both? Only his therapist knew for sure.

By the end of my research I prayed daily for an auto accident or a train wreck that would make Barry stop asking me for more cases. My memorandum, when I finally finished it, was sixty-two pages long. Barry's memorandum to Stanley, which incorporated my cases but presented them in the form of a legal argument, was 140 pages. I do not know why the client needed this information or whether it was ever used.

Other assignments followed, though none as long as Barry's, and they became a predictable routine by the end of my first year. My fear of falling through the cracks dissipated, as did my free time. The routine went like this: Various senior associates would call me into their offices. They'd describe a case, or part of a case, to me. Some legal issue needed researching. A witness refused to proceed with his pretrial examination because, he claimed, he suffered from a mental illness. Could we cross-examine his doctor about the condition? Could a corporation, whose only contact with New York State was sending a letter reneging on a deal to another corporation in New York, be sued in New York State? Does a ten-month delay in asserting that a contract has been entered into under duress waive the defense? My conclusions, to the extent I reached any, were to be written up in a memorandum, which the senior associates would then incorporate into a legal brief or a larger memorandum.

These assignments were supposed to come through the assigning partner, but many times lawyers requested certain associates or simply circumvented the assigning partner and went directly to the associate, as Barry did. Technically, associates were assigned to individual cases, as I had been on the Consolidated trial, but again, in practice, associates—especially junior ones—often worked on discrete projects for a variety of cases. Later, when I had been assigned to another case, the research projects came through the senior associates supervising the case and always involved emergencies that arose during the long course of litigation.

In law school I had learned one practical skill. Because I competed in the Moot Court competition, and my team eventually won, I spent many hours researching case law in the library. The ability to track down relevant legal precedent was not required for graduation. But fortunately for me, by the time I arrived at C & C, I was well equipped to toil beneath the library's fluorescent lights, ink smears on my fingertips, an unhealthy shine to my forehead. Sometimes the senior associate had already found one case, which gave me a head start. Using a "key" numbering system established by the law book publisher, I could locate the paragraph in the case that contained the relevant conclusion, and cross-reference it in a digest with other jurisdictions and other cases. Or, if I didn't have a case, I could look at the digest index under "Duress" or "Waiver" and hope that I would find a section that sounded relevant. I could also use the computer and construct a search on a legal database for all occurrences of the word "duress" within three words of "waiver" or "waive." My hope, of course, was that the search did not turn up

proper elements of its complaint? Do all the written questions and document requests propounded by the lawyers need to be answered as asked? What I was litigating was often lost on me, unless it was the right to litigate in the first place. To litigate for the pure love of litigation.

Night. C & C's "overtime coordinator" makes her rounds. She wants to know who needs secretarial and word-processing time, who's staying for dinner. She takes orders from the associates on my floor. Daniel and Jay are staying. So is Elizabeth. They want Italian. Am I in?

I do not want to be known as The Man Who Disappears Before Dinner. There is always another case to be read, another jurisdiction to be reviewed. If the law is settled in Massachusetts, it might be unsettled in New Hampshire, to say nothing of Vermont. Because no case is ever exactly the same, the research possibilities are practically infinite. In law school I had always been a finite guy, rushing to conclusions without the thoroughness of some of my classmates. It was a scholastic strategy that had served me well; I got decent grades while saving time for the things I loved like running, reading, music, friends. Life was about finding a sensible balance, I reasoned. Man does not live by work alone. But now the balance was shifting, propelled by forces beyond my control that favored the infinite, that would not rest until every jurisdiction had been plumbed and its fruits extracted, regardless of cost.

We gather in the twenty-eighth-floor conference room, the newly annointed and freshly scrubbed. Outside, the marathon has come and gone without our participation, but inside it's just beginning. Elizabeth tells us it's going to be another long night. Daniel rolls his eyes. "Get a life," he says, as if he has one. Elizabeth compresses her salad greens to make them look as if some have been eaten. She's used to Daniel's quips. They have been eating together nearly every night since their first days at C & C. I am a recent addition; now that I have work and no paralegals with whom to share it I cannot escape their gravitational pull.

Eating dinner with this group is "face time." It is the first checkpoint in a night that ends with a delivery to Word Processing and a dial-a-car. If you miss dinner you will acquire a reputation as a slacker, a shirker, a family man. Word will leak back to the partners that you left early. The partners, you imagine, will wonder why you had so little work to do that you could afford to have dinner at home. They will notice all the hours attributed to Legal Education on your time sheets. Perhaps you aren't as meticulous as Daniel or Jay or the others who stay late. Perhaps they made a mistake in hiring you. You obviously gave more weight to your social calendar than the job you've been hired to do. What is wrong with you? Do you have a life?

"Are you going to eat that or just play with it?" Daniel asks Elizabeth.

"I'm eating," says Elizabeth. "I'm not hungry."

"I'm ordering you a steak," says Daniel as he reaches for the telephone.

"Daniel, don't," cries Elizabeth.

Daniel pretends to dial a number. Elizabeth grabs his wrist. Her pale and skinny hand, ringless, unadorned, remains on Daniel's arm for a few seconds more than is necessary to prevent him from calling. Daniel shrugs and hangs up the telephone.

"You'd love it," he says.

"Gross, Daniel," says Elizabeth.

Jay, who has been reading from a thick velobound document, says, "Could you lovebirds keep it down?"

Daniel frowns. Elizabeth blushes. The other associates at the table snicker. Yet we all know Daniel isn't interested in Elizabeth: he's

Which of these associates have homes?

I glance around the table and count wedding bands. Two out of ten. But both their spouses are also lawyers, probably enjoying a fine Italian meal in the comfort of their own conference rooms. No one else seems anxious to leave. They linger over their meals, rummaging through the mountains of paper, utensils, and tins for hidden treats. Unlike the lunch hour, when everyone inhales their food, the associates here appear to have all the time in the world.

Daniel does not look at Elizabeth. Elizabeth does not look at Jay. Jay doesn't look at anyone. I observe the soap opera, changing channels on the client's dime.

Across from the library near main reception was the partners' bathroom, an architectural quirk from a previous occupant or perhaps a deliberate design for visiting guests. Though it was not strictly reserved for partners, associates rarely used it. Unlike the other bathrooms, it had a single stall, a urinal, and a shower, and could be locked from the inside. Darkly tiled in burgundy and navy, with a row of bottled ablutions lining the sink, it had a masculine sort of elegance. No one knew how it came to be the partners' bathroom, but the name stuck, and few associates would venture into it for fear of encountering a partner in close quarters.

I had been researching "alter ego" cases for a week when I paid my first visit, driven there by desperation and its proximity to the library. Once I was inside, its cocoonlike ambience soothed me, and I spent the better part of a half hour poking among the vials along the sink. With the door locked, I had no fear I would be interrupted. I realized that its inaccessibility to the outside world was as much a virtue for the partners as for the associates. In a firm that closely guarded your presence, absence was a valuable commodity. The bathroom was a mystery, a secret within a secret. Its dark luxury like an elegant riddle.

After that initial foray, I realized I could run to work in the morning and shower in the partners' bathroom. By running home one night and running to work early the next morning, I could avoid accumulating suits in my office. This required wearing yesterday's shirt, and sometimes the same suit and tie, but I didn't mind and no one else seemed to notice. Many women kept multiple pairs of shoes in their desk drawers; I reasoned I could keep a few dirty shirts hanging behind my door.

As I padded from partners' bathroom to my office, I was greeted by the regular and orderly sight of closed doors and darkened office suites. Printers and fax machines idled silently, tiny crystals illuminating their "standby" mode. No phones rang; no computers chirped. A door ajar, or an illuminated light, felt like a hole in the fabric of the universe, a torn curtain through which entropy poured. Daniel's office was always one of those holes.

At first, I wondered why he didn't simply shut off his light when he left for the night. He knew the cleaning crews had long since finished their appointed rounds. But then I noticed other offices, other open doors and burning lights, and I realized that the lack of energy conservation represented a conscious effort, not an indifference to the plight of an economy dependent on foreign oil.

If Daniel shut off his light, closed his door, and went home, who would know he stayed later than the cleaning crews? Who would know on Monday morning that he had worked all weekend? One or two partners would review his billable hours, but the associates, his competition for partnership, would labor away, ignorant of his lead on the hourly scorecard. Daniel needed to dampen their enthu-siasm, to use the tricks of psychological warfare to beat them back and, in the process, to prop up his own ego. Though he often arrived as late as eleven in the morning, he always stayed late. His burning lights were like the ski-lift tags kids wore on their winter coats, so

year." Neither Jay nor Daniel was so crass as to say what was really on his mind, or to ask me straight out how many hours I had billed, but that was the clear subtext of my conversations with Jay, and Daniel's ever-lit office. Like a dog at a hydrant, they wanted to stake their territory. They also wanted to know what the other dogs were doing.

I told myself that if I met my yearly goal of two thousand billable hours, I would earn $300,000 for the firm, more than three times my salary. But I couldn't help feeling insecure. Someone like Jay, if he really billed three thousand hours, earned $150,000 more for C & C. If the firm "downsized," as had happened at other firms, the economic disparity between my earnings and Jay's would play some role, I believed, in determining who was "downsized." At the end of eight years, if Jay and I were both up for partner, Jay would have billed over a million dollars more than I.

I tried to believe that numbers were not important. If I did good work, I would be recognized. That was the C & C line whenever the question of billable hours was raised. "We're not a sweatshop," one of the partners had told me when I interviewed for a summer job. Still, I worried. Where was Jay's extra work coming from? While I rarely had anything for Jackie, Jay afflicted her with various typing and copying chores. Why did Daniel need to stay so much later than

I? Was he simply inefficient? Or was I lazy? Daniel, Jay, and I were essentially doing the same things—research and writing, and, later, document production and discovery—but they seemed to have more of it.

I began to be a regular at the conference room dinners. The sun would set, the night coordinator would come around, and I'd feel a subtle yet powerful pressure to remain at C & C. I never saw a single partner in the conference room. But that didn't stop me from sensing them right next to me, observing my every absence. So great was this pressure that I would run home with a belly full of pasta through Central Park at eleven or even midnight in order to remain at C & C for dinner. I risked life, limb, and digestive system to avoid being the first to leave the party that wasn't a party. I wasn't the last; but I was never the first.

"Hey, stranger," says a voice behind me in the cafeteria line.

I turn into Abby's rangy blondness. Since our flurry of activity on Consolidated ended, I have not seen her. Weeks can pass in the same building without sight of land.

"Working hard?" she asks.

"Hardly working," I joke, although it is no longer true.

"Me, too," she says. "Is it slow around here, or what?"

It never dawned on me that work could be slow for the firm as a whole. Is there a general lull in lawsuits? Are people becoming more civil?

"I think it's litigation," says Abby. "Corporate is booming."

A slowdown in litigation is not necessarily a bad thing; then again, peace is bad business for the peacemakers.

Abby tells me that both Wilson and Howie have been moved to corporate. She says they're bored.

"I miss it," says Abby. "I like being busy."

I rack my brain, trying to think of some project for Abby. I feel a guilty thrill at the thought of assigning her work, a *frisson* of power. Unfortunately, Barry's present client is a foreign insurer for whom I'm researching the question of whether its assets can be seized by an American court. There is no role for a paralegal, even if I knew exactly what a paralegal did.

Abby asks if I'm eating in the dining room. I had planned to eat lunch at my desk and review some cases, but I take her question as an invitation and join her at a table near the window. My girlfriend will f...

...popular song from the fifties are suing a rap group and their major record label for copyright infringement. The writers claim that the rap, which parodies and lifts lines from the old song, infringes on their copyright. He's working for Paul Jensen, C & C's trademark and copyright litigation partner, recently named one of the top lawyers in New York.

"Wow," says Abby. "Do you need a paralegal?"

I feel a stab of jealousy that Daniel has gotten such an interesting case with a high-profile partner. Is it blind luck, or have the assignment gods smiled upon him, his reward for late nights and thorough research?

"There's years of documents in an archive," offers Daniel.

"Give me a call," says Abby.

Daniel nods as if calling a paralegal were the easiest thing in the world, something he does every day, no big deal. I feel as though I had slept through a class and now it's the final exam and I forgot to buy the book. What have I missed?

All around us burble the murmured voices of important conversations. Theories being advanced, dissected, and reassembled. Two tax partners scrutinize an Internal Revenue Service tome. A flock of corporate associates guffaw at a client indiscretion. The Trusts and Estates group conducts an informal drafting workshop. Somewhere, someone discusses a football game, but they're gossiping about the commissioner, a former big firm partner.

Daniel's hands dismantle a brownie. Abby nibbles on a shaved carrot and avocado sandwich. My denuded plate stares back at me forlornly. I, too, once had a squad of paralegals under my dominion. But they were gone before I knew anything about war, before I was awake to read the instruction manual.

We sit for thirty more minutes while Daniel takes full advantage of the free/not free lunch. There's nothing billable in our discussion, which means thirty more minutes at dinner with Daniel this evening if I want to make my quota. I leave the dining room feeling shorted of time, a third wheel in an incidental conversation.

Elizabeth suggests I conduct my affair with another associate.

Word travels fast, faster even than the truth. What could she be talking about?

"Don't pretend you haven't been hanging around that paralegal, that blonde," she says.

If Elizabeth saw me sitting with Abby she would know the affair was lunch and Daniel was there.

Firm romances should be "horizontal," Elizabeth tells me. Associate-associate is okay. Associate-paralegal or associate-partner is not. Associate-secretary is right out. While C & C has no formal dating policy, unlike some other firms that prohibit intrafirm marriage, "vertical" relationships are frowned upon. Elizabeth recounts the story of a C & C partner who was exposed with a paralegal on a conference room table. The partner was forced to resign. She cannot name either party, but everyone at the firm insists it's true.

If she thinks I'm shocked, she's mistaken. I tell her I heard the same story about a partner at my friend Julia's law firm.

How about the one with the paralegal caught masturbating in his office by a cleaning person? When she ran screaming from the room, the paralegal fled down the hall and into the elevator with his pants still undone. Later, a review of the elevator's security-camera tapes disclosed the identity of the half-dressed paralegal, who was promptly fired.

"Old news," I say.

"The summer associate and the secretary?"

"Where are you getting these stories?" I ask, then admit I've already heard it. After a pickup in a bar, the summer associate switched his identity by giving the secretary a partner's business card.

Fast times at Crowley & Cavanaugh. We sit in our adopted dining room, and

it's the nineties," says Elizabeth resignedly, the bluster of her earlier incarnation suddenly deflated, "but you guys still sleep with your secretaries."

She's right. Despite the vertical rule, two male C & C partners have recently divorced and married younger female associates. A handful of young male associates are quietly dating female paralegals. There is even the rumor of the forbidden associate-secretary affair. But among all these relationships, it is always the men who move down the ladder. *Dating the help* is out of the question for women; for men, it is practically a social obligation.

"You can sleep with your secretary," I offer.

"She's a woman," says Elizabeth.

"Picky, picky."

Elizabeth shakes her head. The tendons in her neck thrum. "It's not like I have a lot of choices," she says.

With over six hundred employees at C & C, most younger than thirty, Elizabeth's choices wouldn't seem too limited. Yet only about one hundred of the employees are male associates near her age. Of those, perhaps half are married. Half of the remaining half are not married for good reasons. Without violating the vertical rule, Elizabeth's choices are actually fairly limited.

"What about me?" I ask, though I'm over my attraction to women with eating disorders.

"You've got a girlfriend," says Elizabeth.

"I do?" I thought my domestic life was a well-kept secret.

"That paralegal . . ."

Kate is sitting in the lobby of my building when I return from work. She's dyed her hair a black so dark it looks blue.

"Kat?" I say, momentarily confused by her revised persona.

"They said you went home," she says by way of explanation.

"I live here," I say, as if to convince myself.

"Have you eaten?"

I leave my athletic bag with the doorman, and walk with her to a nearby diner.

I chatter on about Daniel's recent assignment, the memo I am writing, Julia and Tom's upcoming wedding in Iowa. Kate orders a rare cheeseburger with extra fries.

"Where've you been?" she asks when the waiter has brought our food.

"What do you mean?" I ask.

"You're never in."

"Me?"

"It's like I'm dating your secretary."

Jackie's message pad is practically empty except for messages from Kate, neat reminders on pink paper with the "Will Call Back Later" box checked. She does and we speak by phone nearly every night.

"You haven't been over for weeks," Kate says.

I remind her we spent the weekend before last together.

"I miss you," she says. "I miss you during the week."

"I've been working," I say lamely. "You've been working."

"Come over. We can work together."

How can I explain to Kate that my work isn't like hers? I can't bring manuscripts into bed and edit them, a Hi-Liter tucked behind my ear. I need the library, the computer, access to files. I can't just leave at six-thirty and go home to my girlfriend.

"Why not?" Kate asks.

"Nobody leaves at six-thirty," I say.

"That's not an answer."

"It looks bad."

"Who cares, if you're doing the work?"

"People care," I say. "People notice."

I remember my last conversation with a college friend who became a stockbroker. All he talked about was money, the things he was buying, the things he wanted to buy. His materialism depressed me. This was not the friend I had known. He had become his work. I promised myself that I would never succumb to the same temptation.

"Yes, it's the job," I say, "but it's not me."

"The job you'll have for the rest of your life." She pushes a French fry across her plate, a lone stick of grease. Her wild hair dangles dangerously near the ketchup.

"You don't have to sign in blood."

"But you do have to sacrifice your firstborn."

We both know she is joking, but I assure her no children will be slaughtered in my quest for legal skills.

"It's the big-firm way," I say. They pay us not to protest. Perhaps they should pay our girlfriends.

"I'm not your mother," says Kate. "You can work as hard as you want. I'd just like to see you every now and then."

"How about alternate Tuesdays?"

Kate kicks me beneath the table. She is wearing steel-toed boots.

"Shithead," she says.

"I think you broke my leg," I cry.

"You don't need legs to sit on your ass all day."

"Okay, okay," I say. "You win."

"I'm glad we straightened that out." She smiles, and I wonder why I ever wanted to work late.

"What'd you do to your hair?" I ask.

"Do you like it?"

"I do," I say. I've still got one good leg.

Christmas and the streets rang with holiday cheer. Little children danced gaily in windows festooned with season's greetings. New York, it seemed, had dropped its guard and succumbed to the Christmas spirit. Even C & C hiked up its trousers and partied. Some firms had cut back on the yuletide gala, but not Crowley & Cavanaugh. They'd rented a ballroom at the Waldorf, sent out engraved invitations, hired a band, caterer, open bar, limos to ferry drunks to the far reaches of the archipelago. No spouses, just us family. In a dazzling display of democracy, all C & C employees were treated equally at Christmas. Except for their bonuses, of course.

In my wallet sat a check for $5,000. What had I done to deserve this? Four months of work and I was graced with a full year's bonus. A New Year's present of unequaled largesse. A bonus was part of the package, of course, guaranteed for all employees who made it to the holiday season. But that first year it felt like reaching into an old suit pocket and discovering a wad of cash stuffed there by a favorite uncle.

I knew money didn't grow on trees; it was harvested from the bitter earth. Already I heard choruses of complaint. My law firm colleagues groused about their $2,000-a-month apartments, the $8.95 sandwiches, the $12 cab fares. In the subsequent years, as their salaries climbed well into the one and two hundreds, they griped about the $350 garage for their cars, the high insurance premiums, the $15,000 summer rentals in the Hamptons, the much larger bonuses made by investment bankers. Trapped by a spiral of expectations, they saw little alternative to big-firm life. They bought the apartment, bought the car, bought into an existence of debt and obligation.

But that first Christmas I was still far enough removed from economic reality to imagine spending money without shame. I had lived so long as a student, weighing my last pennies to buy a slice of pizza or the newspaper, constantly broke, that the $5,000 bonus seemed like play money. Every other week $2,000 was electronically depos-

[text obscured]

...y at the prospect of being evaluated. What about all those hours billed to Legal Education in October? What about my outrageous Chinese food receipts? I imagined a dozen scenarios in which I suffered for my sins.

My review was conducted by the assigning partner, a man whose existence I had begun to doubt. He looked down at his desk the entire time he talked to me. I don't know if he was reading from notes, or had some secret message inscribed in the wood, or just couldn't look me in the eye. Nevertheless, he had only good things to say about my work. Apparently, I did an excellent job on the Consolidated trial, and my research and writing skills were of exemplary quality. Barry Katz, in particular, had praised my thoroughness and dogged determination. My bonus was at the top of the range for my class, he told me, and my next year's salary would increase to $93,000.

I left the meeting feeling giddy and lighthearted, and went straight to an electronics store near Grand Central Station, where I purchased the sleekest and finest stereo system C & C's money could buy.

Daniel says he's not going to the Christmas party.

"Don't be a loser," says Jay.

We are hovering in Daniel's office, waiting to leave. The secretaries have already filed out of the building at five o'clock sharp, a parade of red dresses and hair spray. I hope the Waldorf saves some appetizers.   •

"You go," Daniel says. "I'll meet you."

"Oh, no," says Jay, "I know that trick. We're not suffering in silence, waiting for you."

"I have to finish this brief."

"Pshaw," says Jay, without a trace of irony. "No one's going to read it tonight."

"Jensen will."

"He left an hour ago," says Jay.

Daniel shrugs his narrow shoulders. He seems too calm for an associate rushing to finish a draft for a partner. He lacks the crazed eyes, the caked saliva. He's stalling, I realize, waiting for everyone to vanish so he can slip home painlessly.

"We're not moving until you get your jacket on," says Jay, calling Daniel's bluff. "It's Christmas, for chrissakes."

It's not yet Christmas, and Daniel is Jewish, but Jay's religious appeal works. Daniel logs off his computer and rises from his seat.

"This is going to suck," he says.

"Always Mr. Negative," says Jay as we walk toward the elevators. "Be grateful for once in your life."

We've known each other for four months, hardly enough time for Jay to contemplate Daniel's entire life. But we share the instant familiarity of long hours spent occupying the same space, like jurors or disaster victims.

The Waldorf is a short walk, perhaps ten minutes, but we hail a cab. Jay pays and asks for a receipt. C & C will reimburse him, he assures me, which strikes me as ridiculous but I'm sure he's right. I wonder how he acquired this knowledge, and how he asserts it with such confidence. Because of his clerkship he's a second-year associate, a full year advanced on the seniority ladder, yet this doesn't explain his mastery of law firm procedures. His second-year status is a paper designation only; he lacks the experience of other second-year associates who worked at C & C while he clerked. But somehow he knows the important things.

"Welcome to hell," says Daniel as we step inside the hotel ballroom.

"Lighten up," says Jay.

For someone who practically lives in the office, Daniel's antipathy

Mountains of food, gallons of alcohol, circles of attractive young people. I scan the crowd for familiar faces while I wait in a snaking line to the bar. Waiters pass trays of chicken saté, mushroom caps, mini-pizzas and quiches, spanakopita. Bartenders pour Absolut, Stolichnaya, Beefeater, Chivas. With so much to choose, where does one begin? Finally, scotch in hand, I am loosed upon the ballroom.

In one corner a DJ spins Sinatra tunes. In another corner an ice carving in the shape of the scales of justice melts into a frozen Constitution. Everyone is gathered into familiar cliques: paralegals with paralegals, messengers with messengers, associates with associates. White on white, black on black, Asians and Latinos sprinkled uncomfortably among the groups. Even the secretaries, the only racially diverse bunch at the firm, have divided along the color line.

Abby mingles with a pack of paralegals near the iced justice. She shines from among them in a sea-green dress with a single strand of pearls around her long neck. When she notices me, she beckons me over. I drain my scotch, grab a glass of wine from a passing waiter, and zigzag in her direction.

"Great party!" she says enthusiastically.

I'm not sure if she's being ironic, so I tell her I love the ice sculpture in a tone that could be construed as genuine.

Wilson Holt eyes our exchange suspiciously. I am suddenly conscious of my bearing with Abby and how it must appear to Wilson and the other paralegals. Though their conversation continues, I imagine all ears trained on our voices. To Abby's clan of admirers, I am the interloper attorney who imperils their amorous quest. I am the senior to their freshmen, hanging around the dorm, chatting up the new coeds, offering rides in my convertible. I guzzle my wine and snare another glass.

The DJ segues into a dance beat, a song by Prince that even a lawyer could recognize.

"Dance?" Abby asks, and I agree.

We bump our way to the dance floor, where several senior attorneys have already loosened their ties. They writhe like lava lamps while their bemused secretaries struggle to match their hipless grace. Soon the floor is packed, younger attorneys, paralegals, and support staff pushing the older crowd to the corners.

The alcohol works its beneficent effect. My face feels warm and friendly. I shine down upon the gathered multitude. We are family. Life, love, work, all is one. A triad of messengers hip-hop next to a hopelessly beat-deprived partner. Beside them, Caroline two-steps with Eric. She smiles at me as they pass. Elizabeth links arms with a copy clerk, leaning against him for support. For one day, C & C will doff its hat and bop, forget the strictures that bind us in the office, let the word processor, the dancer from Martha Graham's troupe, take center stage. Her hair fans out behind her as she swoops through the crowd.

As Abby mops her brow, I catch a glimpse of Daniel watching us from across the room. He snaps up an hors d'oeuvre from a nearby tray and pops it in his mouth like a dog treat. When he sees me, he gives me a thumbs-up sign.

Despite the alcohol, the crowded dance floor, the warm holiday spirit, I feel soberness creeping upon me like fatigue; or maybe it is fatigue. My limbs fumble. My feet stumble heavily across the parquet. After another song, Abby excuses herself for the bathroom, and I bid her farewell without regret.

My watch says it is only seven-thirty. Dinner has yet to be served.

An entire evening waits to be destroyed. No one has vomited. No one has insulted a partner. No food has been thrown. All in all, the evening veers toward disappointment. But the night is young.

I wander back toward the cheese table, passing Jensen who is holding forth before a clutch of associates. They laugh uproariously

lost in the rhythm of his revolutions. The song ends, and the DJ spins into something slower. Jackie and her messenger melt into the syncopated groove.

After watching the crowd for a few more minutes, I head for the bathroom, driven there mostly by boredom rather than nature. I pass a bank of telephones, four of which are occupied by men in gray suits. What crisis impels these eager conversations? What problem that can't be resolved in the morning? These are important men, with important things to do. I walk past them quickly.

The bathroom is down a long, dimly lit corridor, the kind that looks romantic in movies but is actually surprisingly dingy for an expensive hotel. Wallpaper peels from the walls. The carpet is stained and worn through in patches. When I'm almost to the end, I realize there are no doors; there is no bathroom. It's a corridor to nowhere. I'm about to turn around when I see a couple at the far corner locked in an embrace, her back to the wall, his knee between her thighs. Blond hair spills over his shoulder; his hair licks like a flame at her neck. Hair that I'd recognize anywhere. Daniel's hair.

I turn abruptly, but not before the woman opens her eyes and sees me.

Abby's eyes are green.

Fraud on the Market

In March a securities class action lawsuit rolled into Crowley & Cavanaugh like an obese cowboy. A class action lawsuit is one of the ugliest and most ungainly inventions of the American legal system. It permits a single plaintiff to sue on behalf of a "class" of persons who have been injured, even if other members of the class have no idea they've been injured. The theory behind a class action is that single plaintiffs, with monetarily small damages, would not have the resources to bring a lawsuit against the entity that damaged them—no lawyer would take a case worth only several hundred dollars. But sometimes real injuries have been suffered. A class action allows all the injured to pool their resources and designate one plaintiff to pursue a remedy.

That's the theory.

In reality, class action lawsuits are a huge boon to the lawyers who bring them. While the injuries suffered by individual members of the class may be small, the total dollar amount of the lawsuit may be huge. The lawyers who represent the class walk off with one third of the recovery. Because companies are frightened at the prospect of huge jury awards, most class actions—if not dismissed at an early stage—are settled. Thus, class members might garner small trinkets like discount vouchers worth ten percent off their next airplane ticket while the lawyers who handled the case receive million-dollar fees. In addition, because of the procedural mechanisms of a class action lawsuit, many times the injured persons don't even know they are part of a lawsuit until they receive notice of a settlement.

are fairly compensated.

A securities class action is not one of them.

Securities are written instruments that indicate ownership or creditorship; for most of us, securities are stocks. Typically, a securities class action is a lawsuit brought on behalf of owners of a stock who have been injured by a drop in the market value of the stock. When a company has a bad day and its stock price falls twenty percent, the next day it will find itself a defendant in five or six securities class action lawsuits.

How does a single drop in price generate so many lawsuits so quickly? The lawsuits are brought by law firms with one eye on the ticker tape and their fingers on the keyboard of their computers. A large drop in stock price triggers an alarm bell. They change a few names in a word-processed document, add the few facts they know, and submit an eighty-page complaint the next day. If the stock price plunged, they reason, it must have been artificially inflated to begin with. The artificial inflation was the result of false statements and misrepresentations made by corporate management—a prospectus or a press release in which some corporate executive boldly stated he expected the company to earn money next quarter. When the truth was learned by the market, the stock reacted accordingly. Thus, all the people who bought the stock at the artificially high level were injured by the company's misrepresentations.

Law firms that sue the securities industry have been very successful in convincing the public and consumer advocacy groups that
securities class actions are an important tool in fighting corporate
fraud. And in one out of a thousand cases, when some executive
truly *has* lied about the company's financial state, they're right. Most
of the time, the law firms race to file the first lawsuit—whoever files
first stands a good chance of being designated lead counsel by the
court—oblivious to the truth, or lies. They scour the records for
someone, anyone, who has purchased ten shares, a dozen shares, of
the offending company, and enlist her as the "named plaintiff."
Then, in this plaintiff's name, they bring suit on behalf of thousands
of other shareholders.

The company, covered by insurance, compensates its shareholders
by making a multimillion-dollar payoff to the lawyers.

"Eric wants to see us," says Daniel, one dull afternoon when the sun
peers from behind the clouds like an invalid.

Except for my review, no partner has asked to see me since I
arrived. Perhaps I am being fired. While it hasn't happened yet at
C & C, there are many stories of young associates called into a
partner's office to be let go, or told the firm was folding. Daniel's
pallid face gives me no clue. On the other hand, a partner would
never fire two associates in the same meeting. Or so I hope.

I follow Daniel down the hall, one half-step behind him. Since
Christmas my days (and nights) have been cluttered with research
projects. In fact, since Consolidated, I have not been officially assigned to another case. Instead, I am a floater, picking up hours
from Barry Katz, Caroline, and several other senior associates. While
Jay defends the rights of bankrupt corporations, and Daniel defends
the rights of copyright infringers, I ply my mercenary trade in any
open harbor.

Daniel is silent. Perhaps he is preparing himself for the big meeting. Communing with his god, the god of precedent. Why did he
get the phone call? I wonder. Why didn't Eric, or Eric's secretary,
call me? After all, I have worked with Eric before, if only indirectly,

while Daniel is an unknown, a stealth associate. I wonder if Jensen has put in a good word on Daniel's behalf. Daniel isn't telling.

His secrecy extends to his private life as well. Though I know Abby saw me in the corridor at the Christmas party, Daniel has not acknowledged my presence. I could reassure him that I'm not the

his secretary's cubicle. Ten seconds of his time, they plead to the secretary. Did he return that phone call, approve that bill, review that document? What should they do now? One by one Eric admits them, listens calmly, one hand on the telephone, the other typing notes on a computer keypad. When the associate of the moment has finished, Eric speaks his order in a simple command. The associate nods, considers another question, but is dismissed by a quick nod of Eric's head and his wandering attention. The third associate backs out of the room, nearly colliding with Daniel and me.

"Come in, come in," says Eric when he sees us standing by the door. His eyes quickly return to his computer screen.

Eric's office is decorated with family mementos and tennis paraphernalia. Racquets, trophies, and plaques line one wall, while photographs and kids' drawings line the other. Two Yale diplomas hang like testimonials behind his head. His desk is empty except for three computers—two laptops and a desktop—and a telephone. He looks as if he's ready to launch a nuclear strike or infiltrate the Swiss banking system.

Eric introduces us to Charlie Rothman, who is leaning against a bookcase, oblivious to the buzzings and goings of the other associates. We know Charlie. Everyone knows Charlie. His brilliance is legendary. Not yet a partner, Charlie has taken command of the most important cases—and won them. If Eric is the boy wonder of the partners, Charlie is the enfant terrible among the associates. He is tall, scraggly, hook-nosed, psoriatic. He had been a Ph.D. candidate at Princeton in economics, the dismal science, before he cashed in his chips for a law degree.

I have a special connection with Charlie, though he doesn't appear to remember. He interviewed me on-campus at Harvard for the C & C summer program. At the time, I was one of 150 students parading through the suite C & C occupied at the Charles Hotel. To handle the crush, C & C brought four interviewers while two younger associates made small talk in the anteroom as we waited for the interview. Conversation was dull and wilted like the flowers set out on the windowsill. Once inside, the interview was not much better. I can't remember what we discussed; Charlie didn't even ask about my grades. I left the interview thinking I would never hear from C & C again. The next day I got a phone call inviting me down to New York.

Eric is explaining our new case. The word "securities" fills me with dread. I'm not even certain I know what a "security" is. Corporations, the class where one is supposed to learn about securities, was my worst grade. The professor was a Marxist who spent his time discussing the faults of a market-driven economy. The exam was capitalism at its most ruthless: only the fittest survived.

Eric and Charlie laugh. Apparently, something funny has been said. Something clever about the market, arbitrage, indexing, hedging. I smile tightly. Daniel's expression does not change.

"The two of you will work with Charlie," says Eric. "He's one of the best."

Charlie nods, acknowledging a fact rather than a compliment.

"Any questions?"

A million. Two million. I am silent.

Eric dismisses us. So many associates, so little time.

"I don't know if you remember . . . ," I say to Charlie as we stride down the hallway.

"I interviewed you," he says, finishing my sentence, as if I were a moron, as if I suffer from Alzheimer's.

"Yes," I say.

"I interviewed a lot of people."

What makes you think you're special?

Our new client was a computer software company that had devel-

but better.

Because so many existing computers and most of the software written for them were already configured for DOS, any new operating system had a tremendous hurdle to leap before being accepted by the public. Few people would buy an operating system that would not run their word-processing program, for example. Our client claimed to have created a system that could run programs configured for DOS and could be easily loaded in their present computer, while performing more quickly and elegantly than Microsoft's current standards. Of course, once he had such an incredible product, he needed more money to market it. He turned, as had so many other sharks before him, to the stock market.

Where else could a company that hasn't even done anything yet print its own money with the approval and practical backing of the United States government? A share of stock is, essentially, like a dollar bill, resting on the same flimsy assumptions; namely, that its issuer will not go belly-up, and that a market for it exists. What is a dollar? If you're hungry, you can't eat it. But you can trade it to someone for bread who believes he will be able to trade it to someone else for gasoline. Once the chain is broken, once the breadmaker looks at the dollar and sees it as a piece of paper and not as a ticket to be exchanged for gasoline, the system crumbles. Dollars work because the United States government says, trust us. And people do.

Consider the corporation. It wants to raise $50 million. It can't borrow the money because no bank will lend it, at least not at a reasonable interest rate. So the corporation gathers its investment bankers and lawyers and proposes a stock offering. It will sell "shares" of itself to the public, in exchange for cold, hard cash. The shares are worthless but for the fact that people believe they are worth something. Imagine: could I go out tomorrow and sell one hundred "shares" of myself for $100 each? I could, if I could convince someone to buy me. Even better, I could sell forty-nine percent of myself, raise $4,900, but keep majority control. Parts of me could be traded in an endless pyramid scheme while I remained intact.

In reality, no one will buy me because no one thinks they can sell me. But when a corporation offers its stock, it comes to market with the tacit approval of the Securities and Exchange Commission, a federal regulatory agency, and the imprimatur of lawyers and banks, most important among them an "underwriter." Generally, the underwriter has already purchased the entire stock offering from the company. For a percentage fee, the underwriter assumes the risk that the stock will not be sold. The actual sale of the stock to the public is then performed by the underwriter, whose presence and financial commitment wraps another warm blanket of security around an empty pocket of air.

Into this circus came our client, TriCom, with its nifty new operating system. TriCom had a plan to sell itself to the public—to print money. At the opening bell its stock sold for $5 a share. Slowly, it began to rise, from 5 to 14 by year's end, to 20 by February, and then it collapsed, tumbling back to 5 before settling, like a demolished building, at 4.

The problem, as alleged, was that TriCom's operating system was no good. In fact, according to an article published in a computer industry publication before the stock offering, the software had so many serious flaws that it couldn't even run programs specifically written for it, let alone programs written for DOS. Nevertheless, the stock went into the market and was a smashing success until nearly a year later when it finally tanked. By that time, TriCom, its lawyers, bankers, and accountants, had been sued.

"Fraud on the market," says Julia.

I bite into my tuna carpaccio sandwich with arugula and walnut mayonnaise. For the

...to plead he relied on something he read or heard that was false, in a securities class action, where the plaintiffs never read a press release or saw a prospectus, they can still bring a lawsuit claiming they were defrauded because the market, which in a perfect world functions perfectly, was defrauded. Investors should be able to rely on a market where stock price accurately and truthfully reflects the value of a company. When misrepresentations cause the price to rise, then fall precipitously, the investors, who relied on the price—not the representations—have been defrauded.

Julia's giant brain stores information not available to the general public. When we were roommates, she knew things—about law firms, legal practices, famous cases—that I didn't even know I didn't know. Listening to her explicate the fraud-on-the-market theory fills me with a growing sense of panic. What else don't I know? Why don't I know it? How will I know what I don't know?

The raw tuna tastes slimy in my mouth. I quickly drink a glass of water, but it fails to wash away the fishy taste. Walnuts and mayonnaise, whose idea was that? Hunger drives a man to strange combinations.

"But the timing is a problem," Julia continues, oblivious to my culinary qualms. "Why did the price rise after the bad press?"

"It moved after the initial offering," I say, not following her reasoning.

"Exactly," she says. "There was negative information in the market, but the stock price rose anyway. There can't be a causal link when the market knows the truth."

I'm still not sure I understand her point, but I nod knowingly.

"At least that's your argument," she concludes. She brushes a strand of hair like hay from her eyes.

"Should we be talking about this?" I ask, suddenly noticing that we are surrounded by men in gray.

"Probably not," Julia says casually.

I try to remember the Rules of Professional Responsibility, something about preserving the confidences of a client. I don't know any confidences; how could I reveal them? Yet Julia, I notice, has never told me about any of her cases. She is years closer to making partner, trusted to keep her mouth shut, while I will be shot at dawn.

"What are you working on?" I ask, trying to shake her.

"The usual," she says.

"Meaning?"

"SEC investigation," she says tersely.

"Who's being investigated?"

Julia rubs one finger along the length of her jawbone, her good Scandinavian ancestral legacy. On our Moot Court team, Julia always had the last word. No matter what the hour, or how many drafts our brief had gone through, Julia would take a chewed pencil to the paragraphs and revise them. Admittedly, her revisions were an improvement, but we resented them. In the dwindling minutes before the deadline, when her teammates were too tired, too weary, too brain-dead to protest, Julia assumed command.

She's lost weight since then, if it's possible, the hollow creases in her cheeks like a river valley. Her lips cracked beneath a thin gloss of lipstick. Marriage has taken off ten pounds and distributed them to her husband.

"I'd tell you," she says, a crooked smile muckling her mouth, "but then I'd have to kill you."

*   *   *

"I was a Marxist, once," says Charlie Rothman. "We were all Marxists."

"Before you sold out," says Daniel.

"Before I got real," says Charlie.

I listen quietly to their exchange. I can't believe Daniel has the nerve to criti...

I'm investing the money for the homeless."

We both know Daniel is joking. One of his ties could feed a family of three for a month.

In law school we learned how to argue any position. It was all part of "thinking like a lawyer," learning to disassociate yourself from the things you knew were true. I came to Harvard believing that abortion was right and pornography wrong. When I left, I understood that if the government could not regulate an individual's interest in her own body, it should not be permitted to regulate that same individual's choice of how to display her body. But my newfound knowledge only saddened me. There was something wrong with a system that transformed strongly held beliefs into doubts, I thought. After Harvard I could never simply believe in something; I always had to see the other side, the counterargument. But now, as I listen to Charlie's and Daniel's banter, I realize that life was never as simple as I once believed. Between an overexuberant developer of software products and a money-hungry class of stock speculators, who claims the moral high ground? Here, there is no dichotomy between reason and passion; there is only reason. Thus, the ultimate wisdom in my professors' paradigms: they made the moral absolutes seem relative in order to make the moral ambiguities easier.

Charlie lays out our strategy. Before the lawsuit gathers steam, we're going to make a "motion to dismiss," which will be accompanied by a "memorandum of law" that supports our position. Essentially, we intend to argue that no matter what facts are discovered, there is no legal basis for the lawsuit. The fraud-on-the-market theory requires a cause-and-effect relationship between misrepresentations and stock price. In this case, Charlie tells us, the industry press had already revealed the problems with TriCom's software. Therefore, the rise in price must have been caused by something else—not the alleged misrepresentations—which breaks the chain of causality and destroys the plaintiffs' theory of the case.

As I listen to Charlie, I realize that Julia had advanced the same argument: if the misrepresentations had no effect on the stock price, plaintiffs can't rely on the fraud-on-the-market theory; without the theory, they have no case. This time, perhaps because it's the second time, I understand enough to ask a question.

"But then why did the price rise?"

Charlie frowns at me. "How should I know?" he snaps. "Speculation. The price of gold. Computer fever. Anything. We don't have to explain it."

"Maybe it took the market time to believe the negative press," I say.

"That's not the theory," Charlie says petulantly. "Information is absorbed by the market instantly. Instantly."

Something about the argument seems counterintuitive. If a company announces it's created an operating system that's compatible with DOS, only better, the stock price would naturally rise in response to this information. A negative review in the industry press might not affect the price until the market believes it, particularly where the company continues to announce the success of its product despite the negative publicity. If, however, over the succeeding weeks and months the original negative press is buttressed by additional articles and consumer complaints, the brokers and dealers who comprise the market might begin to doubt the success of the product, and the company's stock, which had continued to rise, could fall. On a motion to dismiss, where all facts alleged must be assumed to be true, any plausible theory that explains the rise and fall in stock price will support the plaintiffs' claim.

"That's our argument," Charlie concludes. "Love it, or leave it."

Our job, he tells us, and he's not giving us a choice, is to scour the literature and ~~~~~~~~~

~~~~~ in this case from beginning to end, for the long haul.

"You're lucky," he adds.

Who pays the bills?

In the case of TriCom, an insurance company. TriCom had a policy that insured the corporation against allegations of fraud. The insurance company hired C & C to defend TriCom. Because the law, though it has been modified slightly since then, subjected practically everyone involved in the stock offering to potential liability, the plaintiffs also named TriCom's lawyers, bankers, and accountants as defendants. The more "deep pockets," the greater the chance of a big payday for the plaintiffs. The other defendants had their own law firms and, in some cases, their own insurance companies, which paid those bills. The insurance companies themselves hired a second law firm to review the bills from the first law firm and to advise them on the claims. In all, about ten law firms billed time on the defendants' case.

C & C's monthly bill totaled, on average, $50,000. I know this because it soon became my responsibility to prepare the bills that were sent to the insurer. Each bill itemized in painstaking detail every six minutes each lawyer and paralegal spent on the case. For example, my entry for March 21 read: *3.6 hours—researched jurisdictional issues under federal securities laws.* The bills also itemized expenses such as meals/transportation/travel, secretarial overtime, fax and overnight mail delivery, outside messengers, copying charges, court costs, transcript fees, and computer research.

In preparing the bill for the insurance company, I had to review everyone's time entries to make certain they were sufficiently detailed and consistent. Eric, for example, often made notations like "research" or "phone call" without further detail. For those entries, I would call Eric and prompt him to recall specifics. When he couldn't, I would try to resurrect them from what others were working on during the same period. Sometimes Charlie might note a "meeting with E. Foster," but Eric would not note the same meeting. I revised Eric's entry to reflect the meeting. It was not unethical, Charlie told me; in a day divided into a dozen tens, a lawyer couldn't note every meeting, every phone call, every passing issue. As long as someone had noted the meeting, that was enough.

The insurance company bounced the bills for random and erratic reasons. At first, we billed them fifteen cents for copied pages. Their policy was to pay only ten cents. On one bill of $54,000 we charged them $150 for copies when we should have charged them $100. They bounced the entire bill. On another bill I spent $4,000 on computer research they thought should cost have cost $2,000. Eric, who reviewed all the bills before they were finally sent out, agreed to shave $2,000 off the bill.

The dickering over bills gave the insurance company and its lawyers a sense of control over costs. One hundred dollars here, $2,000 there, they could imagine they were saving real money. They couldn't truly control the spiraling costs of litigation, so they focused on what they could: copies, faxes, messenger service, cabs. They knew how much a copy cost, and they wouldn't pay any more. The experience of the eighties, when law firms billed for limousines and extravagant lunches, had left a sour taste in their mouths. But these costs were incidentals; they didn't begin to approach what really inflates the bills: time. How much does it cost to write a summary judgment motion, how much to take a pretrial examination of a witness? Each case is different, every set of facts unique; issues arise that no one could foresee. Should a partner spend twelve hours preparing for a deposition? Should he spend fifty? Could an associate take the deposition instead? Yes, yes, and yes. But a partner with fifty hours of preparation under her belt is better than an associate with ten, or even with fifty. The partner, however, costs $17,500, the associ...

...manage to do nearly as much in far fewer minutes. When everyone bills by the hour, however, the incentive is to drain the last cent in preparation.

This overpreparedness was fueled by the army of junior associates, like me, who were just waiting around for a research project on which to embark. While a small firm or a solo practitioner did not have the luxury of examining every potential issue that might arise in a lawsuit, let alone reducing it to writing, C & C had me, and Daniel, and Jay, and scores of other junior associates whose very purpose was to examine every possible issue and write a memorandum on the subject. Without that ability, we would have nothing to do; indeed, there would be no reason to hire us. Our very presence screamed for work. We were an endless army of soldiers whose generals justified their commands by ordering us into battle.

Thus, for the safety in our numbers, clients paid our exorbitant rates. While none of the issues we researched might ever arise, none of the motions we filed ever succeed, none of the documents we requested reveal anything of value, they might, and that might made right. Because if our clients were not prepared, their adversaries were. It was a high-stakes game of chicken, with each side worried that the other might gain an infinitesimal advantage, the worry stoked by lawyers. And fear ultimately triumphed over good sense and reasonable budgets. Clients hired C & C because they knew no effort would be spared in defending the case. For a small fortune, every possibility would be covered, or so they believed. They wanted economy; but more important, they wanted security. It was not, after all, their money; it belonged to the corporation or its insurer. But it would surely be their jobs if the cases were lost. Thus, despite the tough-guy stance taken by whoever approved the checks, they paid, because they were too scared not to.

Dinner plates circle the conference room like wagons savaged by Indians. It's late. Sane people are sleeping. I tiptoe past Daniel's office as if I'm afraid I might wake him.

"Going home?" he says, looking up.

I shrug casually. "I'm coming in early tomorrow," I say. "I thought I'd get some sleep." My eyes ache from a week of reading thousands of footnotes in law review articles.

"Good idea," he says, as if approving a theory. On his planet sleep, like gravity, is hardly necessary.

"Good night."

"See you tomorrow."

Tomorrow, for him, may be later today. I don't ask.

A black Lincoln Town Car waits on the street as I revolve through the doors. The driver is asleep, a newspaper folded over his face. He startles awake when I open the back door, reaches for something inside his jacket—a gun?—then relaxes. Car service is a luxury that even in this tightwad decade lawyers won't surrender. No sensible person should have to hail a Yellow Cab.

The driver offers me his paper, and I sift through the stories I missed that morning. Subway crashes, murderous children, diabolical cops. The shortwave radio cackles in a babble of tongues. Russian? Armenian? Hungarian? The driver carries on a conversation with the dispatcher, or he's ordering terrorist strikes. I flip the page.

The car cruises up Central Park West, then turns onto my street. I help the driver read the numbers from the front of the buildings. At 257, I tell him to stop. He stops at 323, the next block. I don't argue with him; he doesn't look happy. We're both working late, but he's driving me home. I sign the voucher and skip out onto the street.

It's warm, too warm for March. Two kids sit on a stoop smoking dope. A homeless man pushes a shopping cart toward the river.

I walk back toward the intersection. Another cab slows, honks. I

home in a Lincoln Town Car, ordering meals from any restaurant you choose, commanding the respect of strangers.

Far worse things.

Seven-thirty A.M., sweaty, tattered, my ears chilled with dew, I stagger to the food court in the basement of our building for my morning bagel. Renaldo, behind the counter, asks about my run, clucks when I tell him the mileage. "You should be asleep," he says. "It is not healthy."

I thank him for his concern, and wonder which of us, three-hundred-pound Renaldo or sleep-deprived me, will survive the millennium.

As I walk out, I see Daniel sitting at a nearby table drinking from a Coke bottle. I duck my head, but in that instant he catches my eye and I quickly readjust my face to feign surprise.

"You ran?" he says incredulously.

"Just a little," I say apologetically.

"That's insane."

So is working all night, but I don't tell him.

He asks where I will shower and change, and I tell him about the partners' bathroom, explain my system. He seems impressed, if a little stupefied, at my routine.

"Why breathe more air than you have to in this city?" he asks.

I consider his question seriously. "It's something I've always done," I say after a moment. "I didn't want to give it up."

My answer leaves us both quiet, as if remembering what we have relinquished. Once, we all listened to new music, drank cheap beer, danced with lovers, stayed out until dawn. When we awoke, we hadn't been dreaming of practicing law.

Daniel drains his Coke, slaps both hands on the table. "I left you a memo," he says.

"A memo?"

"It's just a draft. Some cases I found."

The walls close around me. Memo? He wrote a memo? We were supposed to be working together. No one said anything about writing a memo.

"You don't have to read it," he says, as if he thinks I am panicking about time.

I try to play cool, ask him calmly how long it is. If I have a few free minutes maybe I could read it.

He shrugs. He's never been good with numbers. "Thirty pages?" he guesses.

"Thirty pages!"

"Thirty-five pages?"

I have barely begun to collect cases, to read the heavily footnoted law review articles describing the economic analysis underlying the fraud-on-the-market theory. I am weeks away from putting anything in writing. Months from comprehension.

"It's not final," he repeats. "We need more case support, and I left your sections blank."

My sections? Did I have a section?

"The theoretical stuff," he says when I don't respond.

"Yes," I say, swelling with pride at my theoretical expertise, a chance to redeem myself, to stake my contribution to the argument. If I only I could understand what I've been reading.

He looks around at the motley assortment of homeless men who have staked out tables in the public space as soon as the building opened. "Do you always get here so early?" he asks.

"Yes," I lie.

"That's insane," he repeats.

So is working all night, but I don't tell him.

support to the cases

we think are strongest. Daniel refers to it as "our" memorandum, and I don't disagree. I have nothing to show for my efforts but a stack of highlighted law review articles and the memorandum. If he cut me loose and exposed my fraud, I would sail into shark-infested waters without precedent. Surprisingly, he seems to believe I have contributed equally to the memorandum, which means I will share equally in the Fall.

I'm still not certain that I like Daniel, or that I trust him, but as the weekend grinds on, I come to admire him. In part, it's because he seems to like me, and to believe that I work hard. It helps that I've arrived earlier than he on both Saturday and Sunday, and that I look overburdened with a small mountain of law review articles. When we eat lunch and dinner together he floats his legal arguments for my analysis. I try to say intelligent-sounding things, or to keep silent when I know I will betray my ignorance. He listens to my sounds, and seems to regard them favorably. At some point I realize that though he has written most of the memorandum, and done most of the research, I have made enough of a contribution that to claim the memo for his own would be a truly heinous act, an act of which I don't believe he's capable. It's then that I relax.

"We're going to lose," I say.

"I never thought we could win," he says.

"Then why are we doing this?"

Daniel shrugs. His down jacket squeaks like a deflated balloon. He's been wearing it all weekend, protection against an overzealous air-conditioning system. It's odd to see Daniel in his civilian clothes: khakis, white T-shirt, down jacket, hiking boots. He looks surprisingly collegiate, as if he had just ventured out from a fraternity, his eyes squinty and dark, face unshaven, hair like red yarn. He's a deliberate study in contradictions: a lawyer who dresses like a preppy logger, a competitive workaholic who shares credit selflessly, an avowed misanthrope who socializes with his co-workers. Which half is to be trusted? Which half is the real half?

"You've got to make the argument," he says.

For whose sake? I wonder. If TriCom knew the probability of success, would it want to spend $100,000 on the motion? Would the insurance company? Do they know where their money goes? Perhaps they do and they don't care. With millions at stake, what's a hundred thousand? It's all part of the game.

"The cases suck," I say.

Daniel grimaces. I realize I have inadvertently insulted him. It's not the cases that suck, I quickly explain, it's the case law. He's done a great job with bad law. While there are plenty of opinions in which courts have said the market absorbs new information instantly, no courts have ever dismissed a case at the beginning of a lawsuit because the market did not react to negative information. In fact, we've actually found several cases where courts have held that negative information can, over time, affect the stock price even if it has no effect at first. Those cases are distinguishable, Daniel has written, because the negative information did not concern the allegedly fraudulent representations. Still, on a motion to dismiss, before any factual issues have been investigated, courts are reluctant to dispose of cases unless the issues are clear-cut.

"You've read the theory," Daniel pleads. "It's a good argument."

A good argument, an interesting argument, a theoretically challenging argument, a losing argument. Charlie told us we had to "educate" the judge, as if she were credulous and green instead of a federal district court judge with a sterling reputation and years of experience as a securities litigator. *It took six months before the stock price fell.* Is it worth $100,000 to tell her? She won't dismiss the case, not now. Will the mountain of paper we're about to dump on her desk alert her to problems with the lawsuit, or will she just be annoyed at the futili...

...heard the argument from Julia, and before her from my professors, and from other associates quoting partners, mentors, colleagues. It infuses the very air we breathe.

"You said we would lose," I remind him.

"I always say that," he says.

"Our argument doesn't make sense."

"It doesn't have to," he says. "It's the law."

We labored for two more weeks and one weekend on the memo. During that time, we worked on nothing else. Though Daniel had several copyright issues he promised Jensen he would investigate, and I had another reinsurance liability issue that Barry Katz asked me to research, we put all callers on hold while we read through the remaining stack of cases and law review articles. Then we copied and collated, cut and pasted, revised and revamped, until the memo sparkled with brilliance. In the end, I spent seventeen straight days, twelve to eighteen hours a day, most of it billable, on the memorandum. Total cost: $32,000. Daniel's time was about the same.

When we finished, Jackie printed the memo and placed it in an envelope, which a messenger delivered to Charlie's office, five flights above ours. A week later, Charlie chewed up our forty-two pages, digested it, and spat out an entirely new thirty-five-page Memorandum in Support of TriCom Inc.'s Motion to Dismiss Plaintiffs' Complaint or, in the Alternative, for Summary Judgment. It wasn't so much that he revised our memo; he simply wrote a new memo. As I reviewed his draft, circulated for our "comments," I didn't recognize a single sentence from our original version. He used most of the same authorities, and even some of the same quotations, but he arrayed them differently and structured the argument to follow his new order.

His memo was better.

I hated to admit it. My second impulse, after Denial, when I saw that Charlie had rewritten every word, was Anger. He was just stroking his ego, I thought. He couldn't bear to let two first-year associates do his work, and do it well. But after the anger passed, and I read the memo in a more dispassionate moment, I felt Grief that I had disappointed Charlie. I could have done a better job, I thought, if only I had more time, if only I understood the cases better, if only I hadn't let Daniel dictate the argument. Charlie's memo truly was an improvement: cleaner, more persuasive, more closely reasoned. He distilled the important facts from the cases we cited and analogized them succinctly with our facts. He never let the court forget that there was an actual controversy before it: our case.

In retrospect, my confidence was laughable. I had never written a memorandum to be submitted to a court before. My only legal writing experience was in Moot Court and the small research projects of the last year and the previous summer. Charlie was a skilled practitioner who had been writing briefs and memoranda for six years. Clients paid $280 an hour for his time. He should know what he was doing.

Barry Katz had praised Charlie as the best writer at the firm. When he heard I was working with Charlie, he told me how much I would learn. He was right, in part. I learned that Charlie was very bright and I learned that Charlie was a good writer. But I did not learn How to Write like Charlie in Five Easy Steps. My secretary placed a memo in an envelope, had it delivered to Charlie's In box, and, presto, a new memo emerged from his Out box. He left no fingerprints.

Daniel shrugged when I complained about the lack of feedback. "It's not law school," he said. Daniel had more reasons to care than I—about thirty-five more pages of reasons—but he seemed not to. Perhaps it was part of his act: a studied indifference toward what he cared about deeply. I assumed he was still dating Abby, if only from

rechecked, typos caught, copies velobound, supporting documents attached in an appendix. Sometime around two in the morning the chicken salad sandwich I had ordered for dinner at midnight began to churn in my stomach. Food poisoning, I thought. I scurried to the bathroom, just in time to vomit into a urinal. I lay on the tile floor, stomach heaving, eyes watering. If I didn't feel so awful, I could have appreciated the metaphor. The physical manifestation of my emotional state. As it was, I just felt sick. Finally, as I prepared to drag myself out of there, Charlie appeared.

"What are you doing?" he asked, as if I had a choice.

I explained my predicament.

"Do you want to go home?" His tone clearly conveyed that he couldn't imagine anything less appropriate, that whatever malady I suffered was the product of my own indolence and imagination.

So I stayed, and vomited two more times before dawn. Daniel told me I looked green, and Charlie wondered why I had ordered chicken salad. By morning I had a fever of 102, and remained in bed for the rest of the day.

"Did you figure it out?" asks Julia.

We sit outside in a wedge between two buildings that purports to be a park. A waterfall cascades down a brick facing. The only signs of wildlife are the pigeons and the people feeding them.

"Figure what out?"

"Why the stock price rose despite the negative publicity?"

Julia's endless enthusiasm for law scares me. In law school her extracurricular activities consisted of law review and Moot Court. Her idea of a good time was arguing about Civil Procedure in our study group. I wonder if a singular obsession is required to make partner, and what chance you have if you're a normal neurotic. I beg her to talk about something else.

"Seen any good movies lately?" she asks.

I realize I have not been to the movies in weeks, since I first starting working with Daniel. My rare free evenings have been spent on Kate's couch, asleep.

"Has anyone reviewed your work?" I ask.

"Sure. Partners. Associates."

"What did you learn?"

Julia tilts her head and regards me from under her bangs. Her eyelashes are the color of wheat. "Partners are always right," she concludes.

"But how do you know?"

"They say so."

"No." She's misunderstood me. "How do you know what's right? How do you learn?"

"I had a review in December."

I had a review, too, but no one discussed how to revise a memo on the fraud-on-the-market theory, or how to write it in the first place. Instead, I recall vague and encouraging noises about the work I had done on Consolidated, and my bonus.

"It's nice, that bonus," Julia agrees.

I don't disagree. Instead, I tell Julia about the memo, Charlie's revisions, the new and improved version, untouched by human hands.

"You're lucky," she says when I've finished. "You got to write an entire brief."

I didn't think of myself as lucky while I was vomiting in the bathroom, but I suppose I'm one of the few first-year associates, including Julia, who has actually drafted an entire legal brief, albeit with another associate, rather than a single section or a memorandum that was incorporated into a section.

"And my name is on the final version," I add, suddenly swelling with the pride of ownership.

to justify their own lawyers billing for the time to prepare the papers.

Eric argued our motion, though he hadn't written a word. Daniel and I winced when he flubbed his way through several easy questions from the judge. We knew that Charlie would have done a better job, but you don't let a senior associate argue a dispositive motion when the client has paid $100,000. Besides, this was Eric's client; he had the contact with the insurance company that hired C & C. They thought they were paying for his expertise when, in reality, they were paying for his reliance on Charlie's brain. Eric was the partner; he got to play in the sandbox. It would have taken a less vain man to admit that Charlie could have made a better presentation, or even Daniel or I. We, at least, had read all the cases.

In the end, perhaps, it didn't matter. The judge listened patiently to three and a half hours of oral arguments, five different ones, and rebuttals, before she ruled orally from the bench that the motion was denied; the case should proceed.

The partners packed up their briefcases, and their associates hauled them from the room. Over half a million dollars of legal talent to educate the judge. For that much money, we could have enrolled her at six different law schools.

We congratulated Eric. It was a difficult argument; everybody knew it from the start. He did a good job, we lied. There were a lot of hardy shrugs among defense counsel that afternoon. Everyone pretended they knew they would lose. They had given it their best shot; they had educated the judge. They took comfort in a few cryptic words the judge had said about the timing of the fall in price. They felt it hinted at an awareness of the problem. Down the road, they told each other, their arguments would bear fruit. No one could admit we'd been creamed.

Now what? The case loomed before us like a crater. One step, who knew how far we could fall? Why not surrender, pay the money, go home and pull the blankets over our heads? Our consulting economist had told us that securities class actions settle for an amount of money directly proportional to the volume of stock traded, not the merits of the case. Since we knew we would settle the case eventually, why not make the calculation now so we could sleep? Why fight the merits when our own expert believed the merits didn't matter?

But why not fight the merits? At least up to a point. What was the incentive *not to*? On this issue, all parties' interests were aligned. The longer C & C fought on behalf of the client, the more C & C was paid. The longer we fought, the greater chance that the plaintiffs' lawyers could convince a judge to approve their fees. And because C & C's fees were paid out of an insurance policy, with each payment reducing the amount that would be left for settlement, the insurance company had little incentive to insist on a settlement now. Either they paid us $2 million and settled for $8 million, or they paid us $100,000 and settled for $9.9 million. It was the same $10 million for them. As for the client, fighting discouraged future lawsuits, other plaintiffs who thought the company an easy mark, and gave it a public relations talking point—"We will contest the allegations vigorously"—until the company could settle quietly several years from now.

We had made our motion and we had lost, but now we had to go through the motions. We would fight the scope of information released to the plaintiffs; we would fight their access to our witnesses and documents; and, when the time came, we would file a motion for summary judgment, asking the judge to reconsider dismissing the case before trial. All this would take time, lots of time, and lots of money. Even though no one expected the case to go to trial, we believed we had to position ourselves for settlement. Several favorable rulings during the next phase of the case, limitations on what information the plaintiffs received, could affect the range of settlement. Or so we said.

piece. If one associate could do the research, why not two? If one motion might succeed, what about a second? We threw everything into the pot and hoped something would rise. If it didn't, at least our bills would be paid.

At least we would eat.

Discovery

I have watched the great minds of my generation flock to law school like migratory birds blown from their true course by prevailing winds. They landed, stiff-necked and weary, in New York, Washington, Los Angeles, miles from the tropical forests of Venezuela and that anthropology degree.

They thought they could fly.

Few students enter college with all the points on the map plotted. The premeds commit early, because they have to. The prebusiness types drift into economics and psychology classes. The rest, a hodgepodge of majors, whose interests are vaguely creative, wander from art history class to philosophy seminar to life-drawing studio to the British novel until, one day, they metamorphose into nail-biting, neurotic law school applicants.

This transformation may have been more pronounced at Amherst College, my alma mater, where most of the students came from upper-middle-class backgrounds. College is, after all, a playground for the rich and not-yet-famous, where the children of bankers can reinvent themselves as rock musicians, at least for a time. But I believe the law school migration is equally widespread, and peculiar to my generation. Law school has become the graduate school for the great unwashed, the final resting place for a plurality of college graduates without an employable degree.

There are several obvious reasons for this movement. First, a college degree in the humanities is nearly worthless. While our parents were able to find decent employment with a B.A. in English, today

Admissions Test. In fact, some law schools prefer candidates who have literally walked the high wire. At Harvard the law school magazine profiled four new students every year—basketball players, circus acrobats, former spies, but never a boring valedictorian or a Phi Beta Kappa. When a college senior who hasn't majored in economics or biology finds the demands of the "real world" closing in around her, her thoughts naturally turn toward law. If she's artistically inclined, people may tell her that law encourages creativity; if she writes, law requires plenty of that; if she's verbal, so's the law! Soon, law comes to seem like a reasonable career option, especially since her true love—the theater—is dead.

A foolish optimism poses no problem when you are nurtured in the warm belly of your parents' home and then a college dormitory. The world, however, is a cruel place with little regard for the flawed and self-deluded. Everyone loves the arts, but no one wants his daughter to become an artist. The same parents, however, can often be convinced to contribute to law school tuition.

To be fair, there were other options. Not every frustrated artist or vaguely creative person I knew became a lawyer. Some actually became artists. (I can think of two.) Some went to work at record companies, where they struggled for years until succeeding as the head of marketing. Others Went West where they sold their souls to Hollywood and the entertainment industry. And not every lawyer is a failed artist. Some have dreamed of practicing law since they were young enough to argue.

For most, however, the decision to go to law school must be viewed as a combination of fear, coercion, curiosity, self-interest, self-delusion, and entropy. Parents are only partly to blame. In my generation, salaries at big law firms doubled, then doubled again; lawyers star on-screen, in books, and in the public imagination. Yes, we hate them, but we love them, too. Our country is founded upon the rule of law, and lawyers make the rules. They are possessors of arcane knowledge, with secrets about the business of America: business. Unlike doctors, whose jobs are sleep depriving and undercompensated for many years, big-firm lawyers are minted and have earned their first 100K before the average doctor sees a paycheck. They are members of a club that, with luck and the right résumé, might have you as a member.

No one goes to law school at gunpoint. In a perfect world one could win the lottery, marry rich, lack material desires. But the world has never been perfect. The noisy clash between commerce and leisure is not an invention of this generation. Everyone has to work: the flawed, self-deluded, and famous. You look at the world and decide where you fit in, or the world fits you in. You make a guess, take a chance, leap into the void. But it's an educated guess, based on what you know about yourself and the world, which may not be much. Sometimes you guess wrong; sometimes the guess is right, but the world is wrong. In the end, you can change your mind, but you can't change the world.

Thus, law school. Where I was happy. Thus, the law. And everything after that I never felt the same about again.

"Bury them," says Charlie.

Another day, a new case. I review the twenty-two-page Request for Production of Documents that Charlie has handed me. It appears to be a command from a plaintiff in an antitrust and racketeering lawsuit to produce seventy-eight categories of documents relating to its claim that our client has conspired to artificially inflate the prices of automotive parts. Charlie explains that the plaintiff is an auto-maker that believes our client secretly agreed with other manufac-turers of auto parts—its competitors—to raise prices for the parts in violation of the laws meant to foster open competition.

"Fifty million door handles," Charlie continues. "Let them figure

[illegible]

ears like cascading water. Am I going to Detroit with Charlie? Squeezed in next to him on an airplane? Thin and airless conver-sation at thirty thousand feet?

"You won't have to spend the weekend," he assures me. "We'll scope it out. Two days, max. You can bring a paralegal back, if you need one."

The plot thickens like a B-grade horror movie. Two of us are going, but only one of us is coming back. They will find my body beneath a mountain of door handles. Another associate lost in the wild reaches west of the Hudson.

Charlie buzzes his secretary and arranges for two tickets to De-troit, a rental car, and a hotel. Separate rooms, he reminds her. I laugh nervously, avoiding his eyes. I don't want to learn too much about him.

"It's a pit, Detroit," he says. "And the client's a jerk."

"Sounds like fun," I joke.

He looks at me as if I've just praised National Socialism. "Fun?" he repeats. Could I be that starved for amusement? Perhaps they need to give me more work. Or maybe less work and more mileage. "I remember when I thought traveling was fun," he says without humor.

And darkness was upon the earth.

*   *   *

"Detroit," I say to Julia.

"At least it's not Des Moines," she says, and she should know.

"Don't knock Iowa," says Tom to his wife. "My wife is from Iowa."

"No, I'm not." Julia says. "Not that Iowa, anyway. I'm from Iowa City. The People's Republic."

"I thought Cambridge was the People's Republic," says Kate.

"It's the same joke for every college town," Tom reassures her.

I signal the bartender and order another round of drinks. We are downtown, a happy foursome, while the river, dark and poisonous, coils blackly a hundred feet away. The bartender sports a veritable chain-link fence along one ear; a metal ball glints in his tongue. He delivers my drink with a sneer at my tie. It's not one of my favorites.

"I don't know why I feel so lousy," I say, suddenly feeling lousy.

"Detroit," Julia says succinctly.

I'm about to protest, to tell her I don't mind a trip, there are worse things than leaving the office for a week, when I understand the metaphor: Detroit, not as city, but as state of mind. Detroit as the place I will return to over and over again in my legal career. Detroit as an option foreclosed.

"Next time they'll send you to San Francisco," she says. "You'll be much happier."

Julia is one of my closest friends, but she couldn't construct a metaphor with the teacher's manual. For her, San Francisco is, literally, heaven; Des Moines, hell; Detroit, somewhere in between. American cities range across a topography of distinction. For me, the entire country is one big plain on which to practice law.

"Do you like your job?" I ask Julia.

"Sure. Sometimes. Don't you?"

"I'm not sure," I say. Long days, late nights, my labors chewed up and spit out by senior associates without comment. It's an apprenticeship, to be sure, but so far no one's taken much time to teach me anything. The work I've done feels superfluous: databases that aren't used, research memos that disappear into someone's file drawer, briefs that are reconstructed from whole cloth. Hard work is one thing, make-work an entirely different matter. "Maybe I'm not cut out for full employment," I say.

Tom laughs. He has smoker's teeth, though he doesn't smoke; thinning, wispy hair; and a drinker's belly. He is also the only person I know on whom these flaws combine attractively. It helps that he's

Kat, you love it," I remind her.

"They call me an editorial assistant so they can pay me half of what they pay the secretaries. They think I'm too dumb to notice."

"The only reason I became a journalist is I was too lazy to go to law school," says Tom.

"That's not true," says Julia, rushing to her husband's defense.

"I signed up for the LSATs and overslept."

"But now you work all the time," I say.

"See what a stupid decision I made," says Tom.

"All my roommates went to law school," says Kate. "I'm the only one without a real career."

"Publishing is a career," I say.

"Publishing is dead. Don't you know that? No one reads anymore. They just buy the movie rights. We're the minor leagues for Holly-wood studios."

"And all the studios are run by lawyers who hated practicing law," Tom adds.

A sobering silence creeps over the table. "I'm sorry I started this," I say. "Is anybody happy?"

"Julia," says Tom.

As one we turn to Julia, her pale face like an echo in the darkened room.

"It's not a crime," she says.

"You're old-fashioned," says Tom with the confidence of long acquaintance. "You think people should work for a living."

"I like learning a client's business," Julia says. "I like the responsibility. I like solving problems." She takes a long sip from her Tanqueray and tonic, then turns to me. "Isn't that what it's all about?"

I tell her about the hours spent preparing the database that was never used, researching case law for invisible memoranda, writing a motion that became fodder for a senior associate.

"You can't worry about that stuff," she says, waving a lime wedge. "They're paying you to do it. Somebody thinks it's worthwhile."

"But what if it isn't?"

Julia sets down her drink. This is serious business. I have called her legal being into question. She will not allow herself an existential crisis.

"You represent a client," she begins. "The client has been sued. If you think the suit is frivolous you can't choose not to defend it. Blame the people who brought the lawsuit, or blame the system. But the client needs your help. That's your job."

I have had too much to drink. We all have. Julia's patriotic stirrings only make me feel morose. Once upon a time she shared a healthy cynicism for big firms. Get their name on your résumé, she advised, then take the money and run when you have to. Now she sounds like roots are growing where her feet once were.

"You have an ethical obligation to represent that client zealously," she continues. "If you don't, you can bet your adversary will. Your client wants to win. That's the bottom line. Can you look your client in the eye and tell him you did everything you could to win?"

"Even if you've destroyed the rain forest?" Tom asks.

"What is the rain forest? Have you ever seen it? The lawyers on the other side would mow it down to get to you."

It's late. I'm tired. I lack the energy to debate ethics and the proper allocation of resources with Julia. The world is a finite place with a limited amount of time for zealousness. Scientists have yet to discover a cure.

"Damn the rain forest," Tom agrees. "Let's drink."

Kate says she's already drunk. "Somebody should take advantage of me," she adds.

"That's what makes America great," says Tom. "Everyone gets screwed."

"Please, save the conspiracy theories for your newspaper bud-

man used to accommodating someone else's schedule.

We pay our tab. Tom leaves an extravagant tip. The bartender sweeps the loot into a can with the back of a tattooed hand. He does not look at us.

The night air off the Hudson is heavy with the smell of rotting piers and dead fish. Two men in leather chaps breeze past. Julia hugs me while Tom hugs Kate. Then Julia hugs Kate while I hug Tom. We promise to call. We hardly see enough of each other. A ball's arc across the park and yet we practically live in different cities. We wave good-bye as the lights of their cab blink off into the distance.

Kate and I shuffle up the avenue past the tavern where, Kate points out, Dylan Thomas drank himself to death.

Scott Turow's shadow looms over any account of Harvard Law School. His book *One L* has served two decades of law students, not just at Harvard, as a bible of the first-year law school experience. It's time to read another book.

It's not that Turow's report from the front lines is inaccurate, but his observations are dated by a generation. The law students I met at Harvard were a much more ambivalent and cynical bunch than Turow's contemporaries. Turow expressed few misgivings about the wisdom of a career in law. To him, the question was not why go to law school (although in the depths of finals he allowed himself some small rumblings), but how to get through it. His book reads like the notes of a hardy, plucky survivor, a boot-camp memoir. Today, law students have nothing but doubts: about the nobility of their chosen profession, about their interest in it, and about its interest in them. It's no coincidence that so many law students want to write screen-plays or legal thrillers: anything but practice law. Many of them see law as a good background for a career in the entertainment industry; others hope the background will provide a foreground for something else. Few are capitalists. Fewer still are idealists. Almost none want to change the world.

Keep your options open, my parents said. Keep your options open, the career counseling center said. Keep your options open, we told each other. Can you open a door without stepping through it? Once you've stepped through, can you really go back? Though I know lawyers who, finally living out their college fantasies, became Broadway lyricists, screenwriters, television producers, writers, and poets, they didn't go through the door so much as sidestep it. Law was an expensive detour through which they traveled to reach their happy resting place. They could have, and probably should have, avoided law school entirely. As one of them put it, she was meant to have a lawyer, not be one. But they were the exceptions. Most of my classmates, once they went through that door, found it was im-possible to turn around.

For three years I ignored my own doubts. I fit so snugly into an academic routine that I barely breathed. Classes, papers, exams, va-cation. Most of my life had been a variation on these themes. Why shouldn't I find comfort in the familiar?

Law school was a breezy reincarnation of everything that had come before it, with fewer tests and larger classes where one could dive into anonymity. There was little of the terror described by Tu-row, and certainly nothing like that fictionalized by John Osborn in *The Paper Chase*. Professors were, for the most part, liberal (more liberal, even, than their students) and, with one or two exceptions, benevolent and easygoing. Even the professors who tried to frighten us, like the Contracts professor who targeted Julia the first day of class, did so more out of obligation, as if they had read the book and were trying to play the part. We soon saw through their terrorist act. By the middle of the second year, when most of us had jobs lined up for the summer, class attendance dropped dramatically, stu-dents avoided th...

...tucked in a desk drawer. Julia, her pale hair cut in an asym-metrical bob, drank without a curfew or a cutoff. Tom, after several rounds, might be cajoled into dancing, shuffling awkwardly to an off-key bar band. I slept through so many Thursday morning classes I should have received a tuition rebate.

We were young. The law was benevolent and pure. We didn't know how our lives would turn out, yet we were sure only good things would happen.

But sometimes, at the end of the night, as I struggled with my blankets and the sounds of Cambridge street life, the thin notes of doubt would drift into my bed. Three more years of school and I was no closer to discovering whether there was water at the bottom of my leap into law. Soon I would be a lawyer, and though I had very little idea of what that involved, I knew it meant the end of a certain kind of freedom and the luxury of an academic life. Playing lawyer during the summer was fun, but I could only guess what the winter would bring. Give it a chance, I heard my parents say, but the nagging notes remained.

I remembered the first days of law school as I struggled to find my classes, to understand the assignments, to overcome my intimi-dation by people like Julia who seemed to have a better grip on the fundamentals. But by Christmas the unfamiliar had become routine, certainly manageable, entertaining at times. And by the end of three years I was tired of comfort and ready for change. Tired of a lifetime spent in school. The working world beckoned, financial independence, a new profession, a regular paycheck, growing up.

I would never know until I tried.

We fly coach. Charlie is upset. He always flies business class, but on this short hop to Detroit coach is the only option. He thumbs angrily through the in-flight magazine while I try to read the newspaper. I offer him a section, but he shrugs it off. At thirty thousand feet he calls his secretary on the airphone to check for messages. Apparently, there are none, because he returns to the advertisements for travel luggage and portable computers.

I lay the business section on the empty seat between us like an invitation. When we checked in, the travel agent had booked us two adjacent seats. Fortunately, the plane was half empty, sparing me the horror of wedging myself next to Charlie's body. Now the empty seat yawns awkwardly, a reminder that though we are colleagues, we are not friends.

Charlie picks up the newspaper and flips through the market news. "TriCom's up a quarter," he notes.

I noticed. Though the TriCom securities case had entered a quiet phase following the loss of our motion to dismiss, the case still lurked omnipresently. The plaintiffs' lawyers were, no doubt, gearing up for the next phase of the litigation. Yet if the company's software really were flawed, it was interesting that the stock could still rise. Somebody was making money.

"A sucker's born every minute," says Charlie.

"You think it's a scam?" I ask naively.

"They're clients," he warns.

"Maybe we should settle."

Charlie looks disdainfully at me. His lip curls and the dried patches of skin along his nose turn white. He explains you can't toss in the towel every time your client gets sued, even if they've done something wrong, which he's not admitting TriCom did. You have to push the parameters, discover the scope of the wrongdoing, let the system determine the appropriate punishment.

"Criminal lawyers never ask their clients if they're guilty," I offer, one of the few things I remember from my criminal law class.

"Exactly," says Charlie. "That's not your job." In a civil lawsuit, he adds, liability

justice to take its long and twisted course. Perhaps if you're going to be a pawn, it's better to be an expensive one.

Charlie returns to the paper, signaling the end to our conversation. I am content to stretch my legs into the aisle, count the frequent-flier miles. My first trip on C & C's dime—or, rather, the client's dime. I'm happy, also, to be out of the office and away from the endless stream of research memoranda. I am meeting a client, a real, live, actual client, a privilege more frequently reserved for partners and senior associates. I am gathering facts like a collector of trinkets. When I am finished, I will carry them home for the paralegals to display on the shelves.

Detroit is not a metaphor, I think; it's a real city and I am going to it. I close my eyes and enjoy the ride.

Our client is not in Detroit, but in one of the sprawling suburbs that ring the city. You could drive for miles and never actually meet a person. The entire country spreads toward Los Angeles while Los Angeles itself falls into the sea. Maybe we are already in Los Angeles. But for the weather, who could tell?

Charlie refuses directions, as a result of which I get to see a wide swath of this great land of ours. Strip malls and corporate parks. Apartment complexes and multiplexes. Finally, we arrive at Dekor

Industries headquarters. Charlie is in a foul mood when we pull up to the bronzed-windowed building with the phallic logo and stern guard in a booth by the gate. The guard takes forever phoning whomever he needs to phone, and when he finally clears us, Charlie is prepared to admit liability on behalf of Dekor, turn around, and go home.

We park in the visitors' lot, not a single foreign-made car in sight. As we walk to the entrance, I catch our reflection in the bronzed windows. We are dressed in nearly identical gray suits, white shirts, and red ties, and carry black briefcases. Though Charlie's suit is pinstriped and rear-vented, and mine is a ventless Italian cut, I realize that few people would make a distinction. To the world at large, we are lawyers. We might as well be wearing uniforms with our names stenciled on the front and *Crowley & Cavanaugh* printed on the back. *We Defend.*

We sign in at the reception desk, where another guard scrutinizes our handwriting to determine whether we are labor agitators. When he's satisifed that we are, instead, management tools, he issues us visitors' badges with our names misspelled and barely legible. There is some kind of metal sensor embedded at the top of the card. I imagine myself, like Karen Silkwood, setting off a radiation detector as I try to leave the building and being forced into a scalding shower where the skin is rubbed from my body. Later I will be trailed by a mysterious car and forced from the road off a steep incline, my body burned beyond recognition.

A perky woman in a red suit greets us as we start down a gray corridor. Call her Carrie, she says, as if that were her name. She explains that she is Hamilton Williams's assistant, the man we've come to see, the general counsel and executive vice president. She keeps up a steady chatter as we walk up a flight of stairs and out onto a carpeted hallway. Did we have a good trip? Did we have any trouble at the airport? Do we love Michigan? The walls are lined with posters that urge employees to Join the Team, Stay with the Ball, Focus on the Goal.

"Coffee, tea, pop?" asks Carrie when she has delivered us into

Mr. Williams's waiting room. It takes me a second to realize she's offering us soda, not marijuana. These days, I think, anything is possible.

Though it's not yet noon, Charlie asks for a Coke. I choose the mud-flavored coffee.

"Hello, Mr. Williams," I say as I vibrate from his handshake.

"Ham, please," he says.

I'll be damned if I call anybody "Ham," but I nod my head as if acknowledging the reasonableness of his request.

Hamilton corrals us into his office. It's the biggest office I've ever seen. If you tossed a football at the opposite wall you could barely reach it. A line of windows opens onto a view of an enormous tin-roofed warehouse. Golf trophies bedeck the counter beneath the windows. Photographs of blond children so perfect that I suspect he's purchased them ring his nearly empty bookshelves.

Charlie and I sit on a love seat while Hamilton pulls up a chair. He wants to know about New York, C & C, Eric, everything but the case. We chat for about ten minutes until Carrie interrupts him for a phone call. Charlie and I wait awkwardly as he conducts some transaction. Then he apologizes, returns to his chair, and resumes the conversation. After another five minutes Carrie interrupts again, and again he has another extended phone conversation. Each conversation is polite, jocular, but clearly business. Americans making deals. Each time he returns to his chair, he apologizes and picks up the thread of our conversation exactly where he left off. In this way, we spend our morning in Hamilton Williams's office, sitting on the love seat, listening to his phone transactions, resuming our conversation, until it is time for lunch.

Carrie has made reservations in the executive dining room. But when we arrive only one other table is occupied and I wonder why she bothered. A headwaiter directs us to our seats while a busboy quickly pours water. The lunchroom is wood paneled and serene, with watercolors of ducks, geese, and other assorted fowl on the walls. The tables are solid oak, the chairs so heavy I can barely budge mine. Despite the atmosphere, Hamilton does not order a martini; he orders a diet Coke. Charlie orders a regular Coke. I consider completing the holy triumvirate of Coca-Cola products by ordering a cherry Coke, but think better of it and stick with water.

We are well into dessert, a frothy concoction that purports to be tiramisù, when the subject of our trip is finally broached. And even then the discussion is waylaid by rounds of hearty handshakes from a trio of executives who enter the dining room just as Charlie clears his throat. They are vice presidents from some division or other, gray men in gray suits, who, when they hear we are lawyers, make the sign of the cross.

"I didn't do it," says one.

"He did it," says another.

Charlie fakes a tense laugh, and I smile as if my face were painted with quick-drying glue.

"What do you call a thousand lawyers at the bottom of the ocean?" asks the third, emboldened by his colleagues' riotous sense of humor.

We shrug, though I've heard the joke before.

"A good start," he concludes.

More backslapping and hand-pumping ensues until the men finally snort off to their table.

"He didn't mean it," says Hamilton solicitously.

"No one does," says Charlie.

"A smile is your best defense," Hamilton opines.

Charlie slips the document request out of the thick Redweld he's been clutching as if it contained the nuclear codes and lays the request on the table. Hamilton glances at the table of vice presidents and motions for Charlie to keep his voice down.

"We're all a little sensitive about this," he explains.

Charlie says we don't intend to get into the merits of the allegations, or the defense of the case. Right now we're just gathering documents.

"Let's go back to my office," says Hamilton.

Charlie grins

many other tasks. Carrie, however, has done a preliminary search for documents and she can point us in the right direction. As he speaks, his eyes drift toward the window and at the enormous warehouse beyond.

Charlie withdraws the document request from his Redweld again and begins to describe the broad categories of documents the plaintiffs have requested. Carrie pulls out her own version, a copy Charlie faxed Hamilton several weeks ago, that has been highlighted and tabbed. She nods along with Charlie's descriptions.

Charlie explains that for now we're gathering everything vaguely responsive. Later we'll make a determination as to what, exactly, should be turned over and what should be objected to. Essentially, we want to copy every document that has anything to do with eight different auto parts: contracts, invoices, sales agreements, correspondence, everything. These are the documents the plaintiff hopes will prove its case that Dekor secretly agreed with its competitors to raise prices of auto parts to an artificially high level.

After about four minutes, Hamilton claps his hands once and turns to Carrie. "If you need anything," he says, either to Carrie or to us, it's hard to tell, "give a holler."

Charlie looks stricken, as if he has been cut down in his prime. I understand that we are being dismissed, but where to and in what direction, no one says.

"I hope you brought your T-shirts," says Carrie. "It's hotter than a piston in that warehouse."

At Crowley & Cavanaugh it was common practice to bill a client for travel time. When I went to Detroit my "clock" started running the minute I left my apartment. Thus, even though I did not arrive in Hamilton Williams's office until 10:30, I had already billed four hours on the case. While some clients did not pay for travel time, most did, and in fact C & C expected it as a cost of doing business. C & C also expected the client to pay for business-class travel on flights longer than five hours. Though clients have become more cost-conscious and the market for law firms more competitive, C & C still managed to dictate most terms of its retainer agreement. Sometimes C & C would agree to a ten percent discount, or a capped fee, but those situations were unusual. Because of its reputation, C & C could still afford a certain arrogance.

From an associate's perspective, billing for travel is a freebie; not billing for travel, a calamity. If you can bill for travel time, then everything you do, even if it's only reading the newspaper on the airplane, is chargeable to the client. When I went to Detroit, I billed twelve hours that first day, but only eight of those hours were real work. If you can't bill for travel, then all your time in a taxi, in traffic, at the airport, on a plane, in transit to your destination is wasted. Instead of billing twelve hours for an eight-hour day, you bill eight hours for a twelve-hour day. Imagine your unhappiness.

C & C also billed for lunch and all casual conversation with a client. After all, who should pay for my time if Hamilton Williams decided to chat my ear off in the executive dining room? Should C & C provide Hamilton with a free escort service? Should I have to work late one Friday night in order to make up the lost hours? I was evaluating what kind of witness Hamilton would make if the case went to trial, I told myself as I filled out my time sheet. Hamilton had only himself to blame for the bill.

Thus, my twelve-hour day in Detroit was really a four-hour day, discounting travel, meals, inane conversation. Four hours in which

Charlie and I roamed the aisles in a gigantic overheated warehouse searching for documents. Four hours that felt like twelve. Four hours that could have been twelve but, mercifully, were not. That's why I loved travel: the hours were like frequent-flier miles, they accumulated while I sat on my ass.

to an office to a warehouse to a car. Instead, I have to meet Charlie in the lobby for dinner. I check into my room, where I take a hot shower, using all the ablutions left for me on the bathroom sink: soap, shampoo, conditioner, rinse, body bath, hair gel. Then I put the same clothes back on: same underwear, socks, shirt, suit, and tie, as if I never wore anything else. I shine my shoes with the shoe-mitt hanging in the closet. It is still early, so I take a minute to poke through the pamphlets left near my bedside. Visit Detroit. Excursions on the Lake. White Flight from the Urban Core. I am happy in this hotel room: large and luxurious, with a separate alcove containing a desk, chairs, fax machine, and two telephones. Everything a lawyer could want for an extended visit. I leave all the lights burning and head downstairs.

Charlie reads a magazine in the fern-and-wood-chip lobby. He has gotten directions to one of the suburb's finest dining establishments. We retrieve the rental car from an underground attendant and drive silently past buildings with numbers in the tens of thousands. Have we traveled that far from the center or are the addresses an illusion of distance, two zeros added for comfort?

We pull into a shopping mall. The usual stores greet us. The bland homogeneity of America like pasteurization: a forced removal of foreign objects. The restaurant turns out to have been recently reviewed by *The New York Times,* which makes Charlie happy, and he spends a good twenty minutes scrutinizing the menu before settling back to order dinner and a Coke, his sixth or eighth of the day.

Sitting there, listening to Charlie praise the food and criticize Hamilton Williams, I wish I were eating a sandwich in my hotel bed rather than making forced conversation with a co-worker. The thought of room service, an old movie on television, a drink from the mini-bar, telephone calls to long-distance friends, seems much more appealing than the finest dining experience the Detroit suburbs have to offer. Who is this man? I wonder. Why are we forced to socialize? We break bread, raise our glasses, and I don't even like him. I share the large majority of my meals with strangers, a charter member of C & C's breakfast, lunch, and dinner club.

Charlie's face is flushed. He speaks about law like a man enraptured. He tells me his theory of this case, how the laws against racketeering are being perverted by civil plaintiffs seeking treble damages. There's a difference between organized-crime activity and price-fixing, he insists. Besides, sharing information about prices is smart business, not an antitrust violation. I wonder if he has read a book, seen a movie, listened to any good music lately. Is he as unhappy to be with me as I am with him? What if we dispensed with the façade and admitted we'd rather eat takeout alone in our rooms? You're a bore, I'd say, and you're nasty; I don't give a shit about your stupid case or your chances of making partner. I'm going back to my room to watch *The African Queen*. And he'd say, I feel the same way. You're whiny and self-involved; I couldn't care less about your career angst and search for self-fulfillment. Then we'd shake hands and agree that we didn't like each other and that socializing with co-workers was a dumb idea to begin with.

In this way the world would become a better place.

Under the rules of federal and state procedure, each side in a civil lawsuit is required to turn over information requested by the other side relating to all claims and defenses. The information may consist of documents, or testimony from witnesses, or the bases for certain allegations, or anything else that could "lead to the discovery of admissible evidence." Only on television can lawyers summon a surprise witness into the courtroom. In a real trial they would be sanctioned for failing to reveal the identity of the witness in the pretrial "discovery" process and the witness would not be permitted to testify.

For example, if you represent a Very Large Corporation, and you receive a Request for Production of Documents from a plaintiff suing the corporation for antitrust violations, and the request seeks "all documents relating to pricing agreements," something that could easily lead the plaintiff to admissible evidence if, let's say, those agreements showed that your client shared information about prices with its competitors in order to monopolize a market, you will do everything within the rules to resist the request.

First, you will write written objections to the request: *Overbroad; Vague; Not reasonably calculated to lead to the discovery of admissible evidence; Unduly burdensome.* You don't want this plaintiff walking around with copies of your client's sensitive financial information. Second, you will call the attorney for the plaintiff and pretend to be reasonable: your request is too broad, you'll say, what are you really looking for? The plaintiff's lawyer, who is information-poor, will tell you he needs everything; he doesn't want you to make the determination as to what is reasonable. Third, after you've failed to reach any accommodation after a long delay, the plaintiff's attorney will file a motion to compel the production of the documents, which you will oppose. He will accuse you of stonewalling and bad faith; you will accuse him of harassment. The court, after sitting on the motion, will split the baby: some documents for you, some documents for him. Fourth, you will go back to the document request and finely parse the language of the request. What is meant by "pricing agreements"? Internal agreements? Intrasubsidiary agreements? Agreements reached with the outside world? The court's first order will always leave you some wiggle room. (You know the documents, after all; the court does not.) You will decide to interpret "pricing agreements" in its narrowest possible sense consistent with the court's ruling and give the plaintiff only those publicly available documents relating to prices charged for finished goods. The plaintiff's attorney, if he's smart enough, will notice your selective omission and will repeat steps two through four above. At some point in this process, the plaintiff will be sold or go into bankruptcy, and the trustee will settle the case for much less than it's worth.

Or, an alternative scenario: every pricing agreement can't possibly be admissible evidence (your client makes goods, for example, that the plaintiff never purchased). The plaintiff's attorney requests all agreements anyway, knowing that the burden placed upon your client in having to track down all agreements, and the uneasiness of turning every pricing agreement over to this plaintiff, are battle points in a struggle for economic survival. The plaintiff is no David, after all, but an industrial Goliath who uses the weapons of litigation to force your client to reduce its prices. The parties will fight the scope of the discovery request in court, until your client, concerned that it will have to reveal its internal financial data, or beleaguered by the cost of fighting, or both, will capitulate and pay the plaintiff a large sum of money to go away.

The merits of the case—whether, in fact, your client actually fixed prices in violation of the antitrust laws—will never be resolved. *The merits will never even be litigated.* Instead, the parties will spend all their time, effort, and dollars litigating the scope and type of information disclosed in the discovery process. At C & C it would not be an exaggeration to say that eighty percent of all dollars billed on a single case were related to discovery. Hundreds of thousands of dollars to maintain the status quo, to preserve the information-rich at the expense of the information-poor. Thousands of lawyer hours to keep the discovery process as unrevealing as possible. The best minds of a generation thinking of new ways to manipulate, distort, and conceal.

Charlie wants to call it a day.

"We're getting the lay of the land," he explains as we peer down

it now suffered the indignity of a civil lawsuit.

"There's no sense killing ourselves," Charlie continues. "You can take your time next week."

I do not miss his subtle shift in personal pronouns. I stare out across the vast landscape; it could be the Sahara. I'm beginning to miss the library.

"You've done document production before," says Charlie, less a question than a proclamation.

"Once or twice," I lie.

"It's easy," he says. "Bury them with junk, withhold the privileged documents, flag anything that looks dangerous."

I remember the one "deal" I worked on last summer, the matter that convinced me to avoid the corporate department and stick with litigation. We had spent the night at the client's offices, proofreading prospectuses and eating M&M's. The associate who brought me along had me review certain documents. "Due diligence," he called it, which I later learned is when a law firm involved in a deal has reviewed corporate documents and found them to be in order. The client was a large insurance company that was buying, or being bought by, I never figured it out, another insurer. I went into a small room where someone had gathered ten boxes of documents, from who or where or why I did not know, with the instruction to flag anything that "looked bad." I saw thousands of pages of gobbledygook, insurance and business jargon that meant nothing to me. I was looking for documents that said "steal ten million dollars from shareholders" or "defraud investors." Of course, I found no such documents. I was in a panic for much of the night, thinking I might have missed such a document cleverly disguised in business-ese, until I reassured myself that if my job had any meaning, the corporate associate would not have let a summer associate with no training do it. Or so I hoped.

I have a million questions, but each one feels more stupid than the next. Charlie seems to be sneering at me, daring me to ask something ridiculous so he can confirm my incompetence.

"What's dangerous?" I finally manage.

Charlie laughs, his blotchy face turning all different colors of red. "Everything," he says, as if we're sharing a joke. "Any other questions?"

I wonder if the warehouse has an emergency exit. Could I flee through the nearest door and escape into suburban anonymity? Or have the doors been shuttered, nailed shut to prevent premature departures? Decomposing associates molder in the dank and airless corners. I shake my head.

"Good," says Charlie. "Then let's get out of this hellhole."

Here's what you don't learn in law school:

You're in a warehouse. Tin-roofed. Poorly ventilated. Barely lit. You've been deposited here by the enthusiastic assistant of a man with two last names. Good luck, she wished you as she closed the door. You think you heard it lock.

You're looking for documents. Specifically, you're responding to a Request for Production of Documents. This is an evil that lawyers do to each other in the name of "discovery." They ask your client to turn over thousands of pages of documents—memos, reports, letters, brochures, books—anything on paper or magnetic tape that might possibly be relevant to their client's claims against your client. Your client is a corporation. It doesn't have only one file. It has thousands of employees and tens of thousands of files. You have to search each one to weed out relevant documents. That's why you're in this warehouse. Your client keeps old files here.

The enthusiastic assistant has done some work for you. She's isolated rows of files belonging to employees and former employees who might have been involved in the activities leading to the claims

out, you may actually read the document.

If truth be told, you don't actually know what you're doing. No one's explained it to you. You remember reviewing documents that another associate had gathered in another case. But you never saw the gathering process, only the end result, and the associate was gone and forgotten by the time you had your hands in his papers. Now you are that associate. The senior associate who abandoned you in this non-descript and forgotten parcel of the country told you to copy anything remotely relevant and flag the dangerous documents, the ones that discuss secret pacts and hidden arrangments. He told you to call him with any questions. You've tried to be careful, but it's equatorial in this warehouse, and that's when you developed your system.

Here's your terrible mistake, the blunder you will carry with you from your law firm without revealing:

You've made two piles. On the left, a wall of boxes, remotely relevant and innocuous. On the right, a stack of documents. The wall on the left is what you'll send to the overnight copy service, the people whose job is actually more miserable than yours. They'll copy and do something called "Bates stamping" and deliver three times as many boxes to you a week later in New York. The other pile, the smaller pile, is the documents that implicate your client in crimes, antitrust violations, fraud. You've pulled the documents from folders in the boxes and stacked the pages in the pile. You plan to show them to the senior associate. Let him figure out what's criminal and what's merely uncivil. But here's what you realize at the end of two weeks: you have forgotten where they came from.

This is a problem. First, you'll never be able to return the documents to their proper place. Second, the documents, according to the rules for these things, must be copied "as they are kept in the usual course of business." If they are in a folder, the label has to be copied or the folder replicated. If they are in a folder in a box with a label, the same replication must occur. The senior associate will not ask if the folders and boxes were labeled. You will not volunteer this information. The senior associate will eventually produce the documents to the other side and no one will ever suspect what they looked like in their pristine state. Except you.

How could you know this? You learned it accidentally, and too late, from a phone call to a friend with mysterious sources of information. There was no course called Document Production at Harvard. No one explained "Bates stamping" or making multiple copies or reproducing file labels or sitting in a warehouse sweating your ass off. It turns out you'll spend the greater part of your associate life producing documents, reviewing documents, arguing about documents, but no one has bothered to train you in the art of copying and refiling documents or the intricacies of making multiple replicate folders.

Eventually, you'll become an expert. You will command paralegals and associates more junior than you are. You will actually try to teach these skills to the wretched souls who follow in your footsteps. But right now, sitting on a box in that warehouse, the air stinking of mildewed cardboard, miles from another human being, you put your head in your hands and begin to cry.

Summer Time

Summer reared its lazy lion head, bringing weekends in the Hamptons, catered lunches under indoor palms, and the Corporate Challenge, the annual race of passage for corporate America's leaden of foot. On a balmy June evening I ambled to Central Park with thirty other C & C employees, including Jay and Elizabeth, but not Daniel, and several summer associates who had been on the job for less than a month. We wore blue Crowley & Cavanaugh T-shirts with the firm name stenciled on the front and our names on the back. We were team players.

Though the Corporate Challenge paid lip service to participation rather than competition, it was an exercise in pure capitalism. Brightly colored banners girded the park, with corporate names emblazoned across them. Captains with bullhorns barked orders at their hapless teammates. Aerobic warmups were conducted on the pockets of dust and green. The fastest runners and the fastest teams would win Tiffany platters, and advance to a championship race in the fall. Ten thousand runners crowded the starting line, practically trampling each other to get ahead. Both in terms of its glittery promise of equal participation, and its harsh recognition of only the few, the race was a perfect metaphor for corporate America.

I did not anticipate great things. I had been running fairly consistently for months now, alternating mornings with late nights. But when I found myself with the front pack of five runners on the downhill toward the finish behind the Metropolitan Museum of Art, I knew I had a chance to win the race. The other runners had the gaunt, loping stride of marathoners, while I knew I still had the kick of a middle-distance runner. A half-mile from the finish line I took off, and no one went with me. I crossed the tape in 17:20, a better than five-minute pace for the three-and-a-half-mile course.

The next day the race was reported in *The New York Times,* and I was, for one brief instant, a bright and shining advertisement for Crowley & Cavanaugh and its unswerving devotion to excellence, hard work, and time out for fun.

Jay finished in 23:50, nearly two minutes per mile behind. Elizabeth did not finish at all.

"Congratulations."

I look up from the cases I am reading to see Eric standing in my doorway. He smiles easily, his teeth rolling in his mouth, as if dropping by the twenty-eighth floor were the most routine occurrence. His eyes, for the first time, catch mine, and I turn my head from the unaccustomed spotlight.

For a moment, I am confused. Is he congratulating me on the document production in Detroit? Is he kidding? Then he says, "Five-minute pace. You were flying."

"Four fifty-seven," I correct him.

He smiles again, and this time I hold his eyes. He knows that we share this in common. Why beat your opponent in three sets if you can beat him in two?

"Did we ever take you to lunch?" he asks.

I'm not certain if he means the collective "we" or whether he simply prefers to refer to himself in the plural. I tell him Barry Katz and Madeleine Drasher took me out my first day of work. Partners never lunch with new associates once they've been recruited. The job always falls to midlevel associates like Barry and Madeleine. It's cheaper that way, less time away from the office for the higher-billing partners.

"Caroline's made a reservation downstairs," says Eric, referring to an expensive restaurant in the lobby of the building. "Does one o'clock work f—

money. Then he'd take my ass out onto the tennis court and beat it around for an hour or two.

We exchange smiles. His says he may be older but he's still an athletic force. Mine says he could never beat me on the roads, at any age, at any time. Two killers. Two litigators.

His back disappears around the corner, the elbows of his jacket shining, as Jackie glides into my office.

"That guy needs a new suit," she says.

"Jackie," I warn. The walls have ears.

"How much does he make? A million? Two million? You'd think he could get a good suit. An Armani or something."

"Did you say you were getting us coffee?"

"Yes, master."

I return to the cases on my desk. I am researching Dekor's civil liability under RICO, a statute that provides for triple damages. In addition to the civil lawsuit, Dekor faced a possible Department of Justice indictment and a state investigation. The defense of the criminal investigations was supervised by a C & C partner with a white-collar criminal defense background who, in turn, supervised a senior associate like Charlie who, in turn, supervised two junior associates like me.

Meanwhile, Barry Katz kept peppering me with research assignments. I knew enough not to answer my phone when his name lit it up, but that didn't prevent him from waylaying me in the cafeteria, the library, the hallway. His pleas for help had a desperate and illicit quality, as if he had to go on the black market to get the assistance he needed. Was no one else willing to help him? Was he afraid to ask? Perhaps he feared that if he went to the assigning partner, the word would spread that he couldn't handle his work. It was safer to keep ambushing me.

"Excuse me, may I have your autograph?" asks another voice at my door.

Jay invites himself in and sits on the empty chair in front of my desk.

"Everyone's talking about you," he continues. "Winning that race was a smart move. Sports are a big deal around here."

Out on the course, behind the Metropolitan Museum, winning the race for C & C was the furthest thought from my mind. When I moved, I moved because my heart told me to, my legs followed, and my brain came along for the ride.

"Keep winning; they'll make you partner."

If only it were that simple: race your way into the partnership, carry the C & C name like a banner across America.

Jay adjusts his tie, then settles back into the chair.

"I don't know how you do it," he says. "I have no time to train."

The first ominous note, like a dissonant bell, has been struck. No one likes an overachiever, especially the overachievers. First comes victory, then come questions about the victory: whispers about steroids and inflated time sheets. Trophies should appear along your bookshelves like mushrooms, arising magically when the weather changes. But they shouldn't be cultivated.

"I run at midnight," I say, "through the park, after work." It's not always midnight, and it's not always after work, but I know where Jay is heading with his line of questioning, and I'm not going to give him the satisfaction.

Jay seems impressed. He blanches slightly and tugs at his collar. He didn't know he faced such a formidable foe.

"You get out at midnight?" he asks. "No wonder you have time."

First round to him. I am silent in response. He dusts his fingertips across the lapel of his suit jacket, crosses and uncrosses his legs.

"I had to give up the marathon," he continues. "They don't let you bill for it."

"They don't let you bill for the Corporate Challenge, either," I say.

... most amount of time.

"Anyway," he says as he pushes himself out of the chair, "you're an example for all our campers this summer."

The summer associates don't want role models, I protest; they just want interesting work and a free lunch.

"You'll see; soon you'll be on everybody's lunch list."

"As a guest, I hope, not an appetizer."

He grins. "See you on the road."

The way he says it, it's a warning.

A message arrives from Jensen.

Jensen, the fabulous, miraculous, mythical Jensen. What could he possibly want from me?

"He wants to see you," says Jackie, pointing to the box she's marked on the message slip.

"Thanks for your help, Jackie," I say.

She shrugs, bangles jangling. "You asked."

Daniel has been working with Jensen since November. He has met several members of a rock band so famous they are whisked into the building via service elevators. Jensen's clients wear dark sunglasses, have greasy hair, are spotted on Fifth Avenue exiting limousines, appearing at the Grammys. They have lawyers the way other people have socks. Now Jensen wants to see me.

I allow the slightest hope to bloom as I ride the elevator to Jensen's exalted floor. Even the artwork in the hallway reflects his clientele: more mod than modern, radiant beneath the spotlights.

He is on the telephone when I arrive, but he waves me inside and indicates a couch where I should sit. His office is slightly larger than Eric's, two floors higher, with the same southern view of Manhattan. Three Harvard diplomas occupy a prominent space behind his desk: B.A., M.Div., J.D. On both walls there are signed photographs from various entertainers, movie stars, singers, and politicians. A sheet of song lyrics with the composer's thanks scrawled across it rests in a double frame beside the court's order dismissing a copyright claim.

Jensen is in his early fifties, his hair a perfect mane of silver. He is handsome and rugged, his nose slightly crooked in a patrician way, as if his face were too modest to claim perfection. He wears a Hermès tie, a dark blue suit, a cream-colored monogrammed shirt.

He hangs up the phone and beams in my direction.

"Quite a performance," he says.

"Yes," I say. He could mean anything.

"Several clients called this morning."

Was he at a concert, a gallery opening? Have the reviews been that good?

"I ran cross-country in college," he says. "Guys like you killed me."

Suddenly, with a thrill as visceral as gunfire, I realize his clients have been calling about *me*. Jay's prophecy has come true. I will be made partner on the strength of my Corporate Challenge performance, bringing fame and glory to C & C while earning a seven-figure salary.

"I've been meaning to introduce myself," he continues. "I'm Paul Jensen." He rises from his desk and extends one hand. I grab it awkwardly. His grip is practically superhuman. Nearly every bone in my hand feels as if it might break. He releases me, and I fall back into my chair.

"I've got a new lawsuit in London," he says. "Trademark infringement. Would you be interested?"

Is he joking? I would take Jensen's case *pro bono*, for the public good; although why give a freebie when the client will pay $400 an hour for Jensen's time, $180 for mine?

I try to listen attentively while Jensen explains the case. Something about art and detergent and noncompeting use. But all I keep think-

room: *London, Jensen, London, Jensen.*

"What do you recommend for shinsplints?"

If there's one area in which I can teach something to Jensen, it's the treatment of running-related injuries. Ice, I tell him. Plenty of ice, and rest. And avoid hard and unyielding surfaces. They are closer than they appear.

When I return to my office, Mary and Jackie are engaged in an animated discussion. They hover over what looks like a medium-sized animal enshrouded in plastic. It hunkers silently, ominously. Either it's dead or masquerading as a piece of office furniture.

Though it may be pure coincidence, the new chair for my office has arrived nearly a year after I requested it and immediately after I put C & C on the *New York Times* sports pages. Mary monitors the phones. She watches the stairs. She knows who calls, who's in motion. If I've moved up a notch on the partners' scorecard, she can't afford the bad press.

"You said you needed a chair," says Mary.

"It's a little late," Jackie says.

"There were delays."

"I'll say."

I wonder again why I can't emulate Jackie's fearlessness. She knows Mary can't fire her; it's not in Mary's job description. Then again, Mary moves in mysterious ways. A secret potion, a whispered incantation, who knows what demons she stirs into the brew. When you drink, vengeance is hers.

"Do you want me to unpack it?" Mary asks, ignoring Jackie's invitation to battle while shining her most winning smile upon me.

"No, no, no," I protest. Now that she's delivered the goods, I don't want to have to pay homage to her furniture-procuring skill.

Which is why, of course, she remains. She tears into the plastic with surprising vigor. Jackie and I are helpless before her onslaught. Mary chatters gaily as the plastic accumulates behind her. When the chair is unwrapped, she demonstrates the special swivel seat, the gliding rollers, the adjustable backrest and arm support. The finest in blue ersatz leather for her favorite young associate.

"Use it in the best of health," she says.

"You've got to be kidding," says Jackie.

Mary looks genuinely offended. Really, she meant no harm. She was only doing her job, fighting the twin plagues of cheap partners and incompetent furniture salesmen. But then a poisonous scowl passes over her face, as if a spider crawled inside her mouth. A tarantula.

"I'd watch my step," she warns Jackie. "I'm not the only one who thinks you have an attitude."

"Oooh," says Jackie. "I'm afraid."

Jackie's nails click quickly along the edge of my desk, ten switch-blades sharpening. But her eyes, I notice, flit about the room as if measuring an escape route. She doesn't want to face the spider alone.

A week later, fulfilling another of Jay's predictions, I sit in a midtown restaurant eating a piece of tuna as big and rare as a human heart. We are five: Barry Katz, myself, and three summer associates. Madeleine Drasher is expected but, to no one's surprise, she has canceled at the last moment.

It seems like ages since I summered at C & C. Two years, to be exact. Last summer, while I studied for the bar exam, another flock of law students came and went like geraniums, blooming vividly then fading quickly. In a matter of months, many of them will return to C & C as permanent associates. A second flock have arrived, and with them the inevitable gossip among the permanent associates about who is smart, who is dumb, who is arrogant, who polite, who good-looking, and who forgettable. There are fifty to choose from

what it is like to be a first-year associate, and I am the new poster boy for the first-year associate: all work, all play. We are about the same age, but it is as if they are of a different generation, one whose physical attributes include bright eyes and bushy tails. They want to know what the work is like; they want to know whether it is interesting.

There are many possible responses and all of them are lies, and all of them are true. It depends on the frame of reference. Is the work as interesting as traveling to China? Is it as interesting as fractal geometry? If I tell the summer associate that the work, so far, has been fairly boring with a smattering of interesting moments, what will she think? Will she think it is more boring than the work she will get at another big firm? By asking a stupid question she will get a stupid answer, the only answer I can give her, the only answer she probably expects.

I remember an earlier lunch with Daniel where we were served the inevitable question about the quality of the work. Daniel didn't respond directly. Instead, he asked the summer associate why he wanted to go to a big firm in the first place. Everyone laughed nervously, imagining Daniel was joking. But when he repeated his question the kid turned the question around. "Why did *you* go to a big firm?" he asked.

"Because I had to," Daniel said. "I have forty thousand dollars in loans." He stabbed at his food as if it weren't dead yet. "What's your excuse?"

But I lack Daniel's studied cynicism, his deliberate flouting of recruiting etiquette. So this is how I decide to answer: I tell myself that the summer associate doesn't want to know that I am a research drone, a document-production clerk, *that goes without saying*. No law student between her second and third year thinks she's going to be arguing the merits of a case in front of a federal judge. She knows that her early years at a big firm will consist of exactly what I have been doing: research, research, and document production. We're not medical residents, thrown into the emergency room with lives on the line. No client with money would risk its health on an inexperienced associate. When she asks if the work is interesting, she wants to know if it's interesting relative to what first-year associates at other firms are doing. And since I know that my friends and classmates at other big firms do essentially the same work I am doing, I can honestly answer yes, the work is very interesting, and fun, I add for good measure.

"Tell me about your cases," she says, as if she were a psychiatrist.

I can't blame her. She is only doing her job as a summer associate, following the script provided to her by the placement office or some underground guide to law firms. *Young associates are more likely to give you an honest appraisal of their experiences when they're sated on raw tuna.* She wears an outfit that is half skirt, half bulletproof vest, the drapey bottom yielding to a rigid top.

I outline the facts of TriCom and Dekor, both of which involve allegations of fraud and cover-ups and financial swindling. I don't tell her or her two law school classmates that I have recently spent two weeks in a tin-roofed warehouse that stank of decaying cardboard. Instead, I emphasize the client contact and the responsibility.

"It sounds like a good idea for a movie," says one of her compatriots, a pale, ill-shaven redhead.

I protest that the cases lack drama. "No one's even been murdered," I add.

"Not yet," says the redhead, and he laughs.

"David's writing a screenplay," the woman explains.

"Written," he corrects her. "I'm shopping it around."

"Do you have an agent?" I ask. I want nothing more than to deflate his healthy ego. Where do these students come from, brim-ming with

stomach, yet I can barely stay awake to hear the exciting search for liability in Barry's story. No deaths, not even an injury, but plenty of injustice. The search for suspects continues.

After my Corporate Challenge victory, I joined the elite club of C & C eccentrics. There was the lawyer who sported cardigan sweaters, another who hung a Bruce Springsteen poster in his office, a third who raced model cars on the weekends. Each activity was carefully designed to illustrate their individualism but not to offend. A Bruce Springsteen poster was okay, Springsteen himself having become an icon of middle-aged, middle-class rockers, but a poster for Pussy Galore, with naked women on the cover of their postpunk album, was not. The associate on our floor who played indie rock CDs did so only after 5:30. He would loosen his tie, unbutton the top button of his shirt, and crank the music. Before 5:30, even though he never met any clients in the office, such activity was *verboten*.

As with the vertical rule, no one enforced a dress code or a design code or a behavior code, yet the rules were well known and well regulated. Even the exceptions were strictly ordained. A partner could wear khaki trousers and a blue blazer in the summer, but a summer associate who routinely wore the same outfit was not offered a permanent position. No one said it was because he failed the dress code, but his failure to follow the unwritten code was surely seen by the partners as a character flaw.

More often, the code was enforced by associates, as siblings will censure activities they think their parents wouldn't permit. A woman who went without stockings was excoriated by her peers; behind her back and to her face other associates commented on her unsheathed and unseemly legs. Daniel let me know early after my arrival at C & C that my olive-green suit was more appropriate for the beach than the office. When I bought a closet for my running clothes, half the associates on my floor came to watch its installation, and then speculated during many conference room dinners that the partners would make me remove it. But once I won the Corporate Challenge, and my late-night and early-morning running routine became well known, certifying me as a genuine eccentric, the comments about the closet dwindled (and no one made me remove it). On other matters, like my green suit, I quickly reformed.

Many eccentricities involved matters of dress. To wear a nonwhite shirt at C & C was an act of nearly unimaginable (yet acceptable) nuttiness. A yellow shirt would provoke a handful of comments; a pink shirt practically screamed insanity. The same for ties: Hermès was safe; boldly patterned, cartoonish, or flowery skirted the line of decency. Gray suits were for court; blue for bankers. Lapels were narrow; ties wide. Pinstripes were in, but now they were out.

There was a difference, too, between cultivated and genuine eccentricities. Eric often wore the same seersucker suit for days, even in winter, the collar frayed, a yellow stain on one sleeve. His was a fashion mistake, not a fashion statement. One summer afternoon, a midlevel associate on my floor returned from Saks with two $1,500 suits and five pairs of shoes. He was the best-dressed lawyer at C & C, famous for his bow ties, his impeccably tailored suits, his handmade shirts. Yet behind his back, associates gossiped that he spent too much on clothing, he thought he was a partner. (The irony, of course, was that partners often wore stained, cheap, and shiny-elbowed suits, or sometimes didn't wear suits at all.) It was as if he were reminding us how much money we made, which made us uncomfortable. He flaunted our wealth in front of the secretaries, the messengers, the rest of the support staff. He was the walking embodiment of the corporate lifestyle, a television character come to life. No real person could afford his clothes. Not even he. Within a year, the rumor mill said, he owed C & C $5,000 in a loan ...

... recovered the part of my life that was still mine. C & C could make me work all night and all weekend, but when I walked into the music store I was free to buy any CD I wanted. It was in these moments—running, listening to music, spending time with Kate—that I was closest to the person I had imagined I might be before I went to law school. The foolish, romantic part of every college student that never believes the *real world* will ever happen, that it's just a construct invented by his parents for other people. We never lose these foolish moments, they just dwindle to a four-minute song on the radio, a carefully cultivated eccentricity to remind us of who we once were and how it wasn't *lawyer*.

"You are not going to London," says Eric.

He's called me into his office and shut the door. For a moment, I thought he was going to fire me, the façade of our lunch finally crashing down around me. How quickly they forget the free press I've given them, the numerous sports fans who are ringing the switchboard off the hook.

"I talked with Mac and with Jensen and there's too much work for you to take on another case."

Eric has gone right to the top, to James MacKenzie, the firm's managing partner, to veto Jensen's attempted coup.

"Jensen said he needed help," I explain meekly.

Eric waves off my explanation. "He has plenty of help. He just wants another body. But TriCom's heating up and there are depositions in Dekor."

TriCom has been quiet since the loss of our motion to dismiss. We haven't even received a document request. But in the last months new noises have been made by opposing counsel about ratcheting up discovery.

If he needs me, of course, I murmur while lamenting, *London, Jensen, London, Jensen.*

"It's not your problem," Eric says, misreading my disappointment. "Jensen's a poacher. Always has been."

I acknowledge the glimpse he's given me into the secret machinations of partners. The feudal kingdoms where the number of knights you control reveals the size of your castle. Eric couldn't breach Jensen's walls by himself, so he enlisted the help of the firm's largest lord. What lands has he surrendered in exchange, what promises made, what old debt repaid?

"We'll have documents to produce in Boston, depositions in Detroit, and Caroline's getting a new matter. It's on a fast track for trial," Eric continues.

In a single moment I have been removed from a case, placed on a new one, and given a revised set of marching orders in my old ones. I am dizzy with change. I hardly know what to think. Boston can mean only TriCom. Detroit is Dekor. A new matter could mean anything.

"You did good work with Caroline on Consolidated," he says. "We thought you'd work well together again. She'll tell you about it."

I nod grimly. I don't remember working well with Caroline on Consolidated. She gave me a pile of documents, with vague instructions, and left me in a conference room after the case had settled. Now she's been swapped for Jensen. I feel as if I've traded my Mercedes for a Honda.

Meanwhile, though we're both working on TriCom, Daniel somehow manages to continue working for Jensen. Who made these terrible deals? I should fire my agent, replace my general manager. Unfortunately, I can't even request arbitration.

"This is a vote of confidence," Eric reassures me. "We think you're capable of great things."

"Thanks," I say as if I mean it.

As I trudge

..., Jay, Elizabeth, and I make our way to the thirty-fifth-floor conference room to say good-bye to Abigail Robideau, paralegal extraordinaire, future Harvard Law School alumna, Daniel's clandestine love interest, and all-around good guy. The room is packed with associates, paralegals, and a smattering of partners. The summer associates are here, too, always on the prowl for free food.

If Abby had any doubts as to where she sat in the paralegal firmament, this party should firmly erase them. At C & C departures were commonplace, but the method of exiting was not. A partner might get a catered dinner at a restaurant, an associate got lunch, a paralegal merited hors d'oeuvres and beer in a conference room, a secretary rated a cake, messengers and mail-room clerks were taken to a bar, where their friends bought rounds.

Here, against the sparkling background of Park Avenue South, there is beer *and* wine, hors d'oeuvres, and a chef who slices great slabs of roast beef, ham, and turkey, which the summer associates gobble as if they were war orphans. A partner makes a speech, grants to Abby the mock award of "Best Dressed During Document Production," then presents her a serious check of $500. "To pay for your civil procedure textbook," he jokes.

I hover in a corner with Elizabeth, nursing a beer, feeling the conflicting emotions of someone recently divorced watching a friend marry: joy and skepticism. I remember my thrill at being accepted to Harvard; my father's voice on the telephone, husky with emotion, when he heard the news. I believed I had entered the temple of American fortune, and was now blessed with endless opportunity. Would I become a Supreme Court justice? A famous prosecutor? A film producer? A respected writer? The dreams were naive, contradictory, and inconsistent, but Harvard was supposed to keep my options open. Everything I had dreamed, and more, would blossom before me. But after three years of law school, and a year at C & C, my opportunities don't seem as endless. If I truly wanted to be a film producer, I should have gone to film school. If I wanted to write, I should have found a hovel. As for a seat on the Court or in the famous prosecutor's office, there were plenty of Harvard grads who were far more qualified than I for those positions. Harvard had prepared me best for exactly what I was doing now, just as it would Abby, just as it would the thousands who came after her.

"You'd think she was your girlfriend," says Elizabeth.

"Your idea, not mine," I remind her.

"Never." Elizabeth swigs her beer. She's getting drunk. When you don't eat, the drinking is cheaper.

At eight, Abby's party spills out of the firm and into a hotel lounge where the drinking continues. The prices are absurd, eight dollars for a mixed drink, twelve for a name brand, but the associates fall over each other in their eagerness to play big spender. Someone gives the waitress a credit card, and soon we can't even make her take our cash. With Abby, and two handfuls of summer associates in our midst, this entire night is on C & C, and we know it. Food arrives; the drinks grow more outrageous: Harvey Wallbangers, Fuzzy Navels, Sex on the Beach. Three- and four-liquor concoctions that are half-drunk and forgotten.

Cigars are dispensed. Dial-a-cars are called. We squeeze into them for a bar owned by a summer associate's girlfriend's brother's college roommate. In the backseat, Elizabeth rests her head on my shoulder. She is very drunk; so am I. I keep reminding myself I should call Kate, but I can never find a telephone. There is a cellular phone in the car, but another associate is having a heated discussion on it with someone about the Yankees.

We lurch downtown, Elizabeth's head flopping against my shoulder like a beach ball. Her thigh is pressed tightly against mine. Or maybe it's my thigh pressed against hers. Or maybe it's someone

efforts. He thanks me profusely, as if it were my money. He tells me he'd like to work with me before he returns to school. I think he is confusing me with someone else. I promise I'll call him in the morning, then promptly forget both his name and his face.

TriBeCa. SoHo. NoHo. At each stop we lose a few stragglers, but as long as we have Abby and, more important, at least one summer associate, we're on the gravy train. I remember the Australian associate who took me with him for weekly summer lunches. Was it me, or was it the free lunch? Now I am coloring the season for these associates. They will rate C & C's summer program as one of the best. Hard work and time out for fun. They will believe it.

At two A.M. I find myself on the Bowery with the remaining nucleus of young associates, summer associates, and paralegals, lurching across a bar. One of the last visions I remember, before I somehow make my way home, is Abby on Daniel's lap, hands entwined, their romance out in the open for all the firm to see.

"Killer summer," says Jay as he plops himself into the chair by my door.

"Make yourself comfortable," I say, because I know he will.

"Three hundred twenty-two hours." He holds up his monthly time sheet like a blue ribbon.

"How is that possible?" I ask.

"It's not like I'm double billing," he says defensively.

Recently, another lawyer at a big firm was brought up on ethics charges for billing two clients for the same work. There are rules against these things, meant to prevent lawyers from taking advantage of their ignorant clients, and to discourage bad habits. In an environment where travel time is billable, where the same legal issues arise in different cases, where multiple associates are assigned to the same matter, the opportunity to double bill is ever-present. Though no one would admit to the practice, it's easy to see how, in the race for hours, two associates could be assigned to do the work of one, two associates could research one question for different clients, one associate could bill a second client while traveling for the first. It's not called double billing if the work is actually done.

"It's been a good summer for you, too," Jay adds magnanimously. "Won the Corporate Challenge. Got dinged by Jensen."

Jensen's passivity doesn't count as active rejection, I think but don't say. Instead, I remind myself in the future not to share my private disappointments with the public. Especially a critical public.

"The summer associates love that stuff," he says. "They think all we do is run and go out to lunch. They don't know the partners couldn't care less about personalities."

I know Jay is trying to shake me, to revise his forecast about my success now that my fortunes have dimmed. I've had a moment of glory; now it's his turn to kick down the homestretch. I understand his need to shine, his insecurity. I understand, yet I am shaken.

"Don't worry," he says, rising from his seat. "I hear Jensen's a jerk. And they always need someone to impress summer associates. When your legs go, they'll just usher you quietly out the back door."

He cackles all the way back to his office, leaving me in his wake like a discarded shoe.

Three hundred twenty-two hours, I think. Back-to-back marathons, weekend after weekend, month after month, year to year. The race is not to the swift; anyone can sprint a few miles. No, the race is to the plodding dullards, pounding their heads to the floor, night after night, their brows thick with bone, their brains soft with paper. Jay will beat me down eventually. He'll leave me on the hill, grateful for the view of his backside, happy to be standing anywhere at all. I never had a chance.

Uncommon Interest

The documents arrived in droves like herded cattle. First, there were the boxes sent to us from Detroit in the Dekor Industries case. They were deposited in a "war room," where they were reviewed by Charlie, then coded by paralegals who described each document and its range of Bates numbers, then copied again and shipped off by messenger to opposing counsel. Then there were TriCom's boxes: reams and reams of draft filings with the Securities and Exchange Commission relating to the sale of TriCom stock sent to us by TriCom's investment bankers. The TriCom plaintiffs had made their first document request, and it was massive, rivaled only by our objections to it.

Though the TriCom plaintiffs had specifically demanded the SEC documents, Eric and Charlie decided to object to their request because the various drafts had been prepared or reviewed by lawyers; therefore, they were subject to an attorney-client privilege. The attorney-client privilege, broadly speaking, protects communications from a client to a lawyer, and the lawyer's legal advice to the client, from disclosure. Eric and Charlie reasoned that a draft SEC filing reflected TriCom's communication with its attorneys and any notes or markups on the draft reflected the attorneys' legal advice to TriCom.

There was one problem with their argument: even if the advice was *legal* advice, rather than business advice, the attorney-client privilege is waived if the communication is shared with a third party. In the case of draft SEC fili...

...ing so that the SEC would approve the stock offering.

Eric and Charlie thought they could get around this problem by asserting a "common interest" privilege. They intended to argue that the third parties shared a common interest with TriCom and its lawyers such that the communications between and among them should be treated as if they were one entity seeking legal advice. When we received the plaintiffs' document request, we objected to producing entire categories of documents on the grounds of attorney-client privilege. We agreed to produce other documents, subject to limitations, "when they become available." In short, we threw a giant roadblock in front of plaintiffs' orderly march toward trial.

Of course, this was standard defense strategy. Delay, delay, and delay. Plaintiffs, who are injured, want their money as soon as possible. Defendants, who have the money, want to hold on to it as long as possible. C & C got paid whether the case settled in two months or two years. In two years, however, we would be a great deal richer.

Daniel and I were assigned to review the correspondence and drafts of SEC filings, and to prepare a "privilege log," a report listing every document that we claimed was privileged: who wrote it, who received it, and the subject matter. Our objective was to be as vague as possible, to reveal enough about the document so that a judge would support our argument, but not enough so that the plaintiffs would know what was in the document.

Because of our delay in producing documents, and our objection to producing draft filings, the plaintiffs requested the judge to assign a magistrate to oversee discovery. The judge was more than happy to do so. A federal judge, with impeccable credentials, does not want to be dragged into the mud with the cats. She didn't spend fifteen years as a partner at a powerful Wall Street firm and another ten as a major contributor to the Democratic party to referee a spitball fight. Fortunately for her, the rules provide a mechanism for dumping this unsavory aspect of litigation onto a magistrate.

One rainy day in October Charlie and I trudged down to the federal courthouse on Centre Street in lower Manhattan, where we met our magistrate and discussed our business. It was my first time in such close proximity to Justice. I carried a briefcase full of case law for Charlie. The magistrate listened to our positions, and then instructed us to submit our privilege log and our written arguments detailing why the documents should be withheld. He bluntly told us that he didn't think our position had much merit, but he would read and review our arguments carefully. He also told us that he was concerned with the pace of discovery. Why had no other documents been produced? Why had no depositions been scheduled? What was taking so long? The usual blather, Charlie said, in the cab ride back to the office. Because of the number of documents, the magistrate gave us sixty days to prepare the log and our argument. Sixty days longer than the plaintiffs said we needed. Sixty more days to rack up the bills.

"Saddle up," says Charlie.

The insurance man is coming to town and we're dragging out the dogs and ponies.

Now that we've hunkered down on TriCom, the insurance company has retained a law firm—"coverage counsel"—to check up on its law firm. Why spend fifty thousand a month when you can spend one hundred thousand?

"Today is a TriCom day," Charlie instructs. "Nobody should be doing anything else."

I join Daniel and Wilson Holt in the conference room set aside

oune yet to materialize, there are no other boxes for me to hide behind. Daniel, too, is still occupied by Jensen, though I've noted gleefully that his work seems to consist mostly of library research.

I set up shop next to the documents, paper and pencil before me, a perplexed expression affixed to my face. I have never prepared a privilege log and have no idea where to start. Daniel, however, from his summer at another firm where they made him do real work, does. He gives me preprinted sheets on which I'm supposed to list the date, author, recipient, subject matter, and other salient information about each document. We will then give our scrawlings to Jackie, who will type the information into a more readable form. Daniel's access to arcane information reminds me of Julia, and again I wonder why certain people know things that other people don't even know they don't know. Does my lack of knowledge reflect my true affinity for law or does it simply reflect their neurosis? Is their calling divine while mine merely mundane? There are no answers to these questions, no secret incantations to whisper over a crystal ball. Hope, however, and ambivalence, spring eternal.

The insurance lawyer is duly impressed. He waddles about the room, poking at boxes, pursing his lips, and looking enthralled. His law firm often handles cases too small for C & C; they depend on referrals, the kindness of strangers. To rock the boat would threaten him with drowning. He mutters a few words about the securities industry, the need for reform, the high cost of defense. "It's corporate bingo," he grouses. "Damn lotto for lawyers." Eric and Charlie agree, while I try to smile and Daniel frowns deeply. Wilson Holt ignores everybody, his eyes locked on his laptop computer.

The insurance lawyer asks about our plans, and I listen closely. I want to know how many weekends I will be working, whether I will have time to spend with Kate. I've got four weeks of vacation and so far I've used one. There are senior associates who are owed entire months, their lost vacations accruing like an inheritance: you can't take it with you. Eric says we need to speed up the document collection, review the draft SEC filings, prepare the privilege argument. There are depositions to consider, witnesses to interview, a computer expert to be retained. A trip to Boston is not out of the question.

"This is a very big case," Eric concludes.

"You're doing great work," says the insurance man. "Anyone ready to eat?"

I look to Daniel who looks at Eric who ignores us. It's late; he's famished; it's been hours since his last breakfast meeting. "Great idea," he says, and Charlie agrees. They stroll from the room, insurance man in tow, next stop lunch.

Wilson looks up from his computer. "I guess Eric didn't mean us," he says.

"Why should he?" asks Daniel. "Then he'd have to pay for us."

But he's wrong about one thing. Later, when I review the bills, I see that the insurance company has paid for lunch—the meal and the time spent eating it.

"What a waste," says Kate.

We are sitting on the floor in her studio apartment. Outside, the trucks rattle down Broadway on their way to the nether reaches of lower Manhattan. Winter's in the air, though fall has just arrived, the kind of Saturday in college I'd have spent at football games and postgame parties. Now I am preparing to leave for the office.

"The magistrate gave us sixty days," I tell her.

"Why can't they just take your word?"

The whole point of litigation, I explain to Kate, is to fight about everything. Without the fight, the lion would lie down with the lamb, and litigators would be relegated to cleaning their cages.

"That's dumb," says Kate.

The hours are a lot better in-house," I agree.

"What's in-house?"

I explain that "in-house" means a company's own legal staff, as opposed to outside counsel that the company hires for specific projects.

"Can you get one of those jobs?" asks Kate.

"They don't pay as much."

"More than an editorial assistant?" It's a rhetorical question, I know.

"They don't hire right out of law school."

"You're not right out of law school."

"Almost."

"What do you have to lose?"

"I'm not ready to leave, yet, Kat," I say.

"You're always complaining about the hours, how boring the work is."

"I am?"

"You are."

It's true I've vented once or twice or six times to Kate, but I considered that part of the normal "everyone hates his job" colloquy. I'm an associate; I'm supposed to be overworked and overpaid. Thinking back on it, however, I realize I spend more time complaining about my job than Kate does; in fact, except for our night on the town with Julia and Tom, I've never heard Kate complain. And then it was about the money, not the work.

Perhaps Kate knows me better than I know myself. As I look at her Cheshire cat grin, threatening to swallow her whole, I know she thinks she does. She'd work all night for pennies if someone gave her a manuscript she loved. So would I, but the only tomes I've reviewed don't generate strong emotions. That's why they pay me instead. Sometimes we are the last to discover a truth about ourselves that is clear to everyone else. The best hiding place is always the most obvious place: the nose on your face, the palm of your hand. We uncurl our fingers and the truth tumbles out.

"Maybe you're right," I admit. "But I've still got to write this privilege log."

"And I still think it's a waste of time."

"That's why they pay me the big bucks," I say.

Kate gives me a perfunctory kiss farewell. "Bring something home for dinner," she adds.

Kate's refrigerator is crowded with takeout tins of unclaimed food I've purloined from C & C conference room dinners. She reaps the benefit of staying late, without staying late. Tonight, though, I promise to return before the leftovers.

"This friend," I ask, "whose girlfriend works in-house. He's a guy?"

"Jealous?" she asks.

"Just curious," I lie.

"Actually," she says, with that grin again, "he's an old boyfriend."

Sometimes, I think, it's better not to ask.

"It's dead," says Jackie, a week later. "You killed my computer."

I accompany her to her secretarial station, where the privilege log is frozen on her computer screen.

"Dead," she repeats. "As a doorknob."

I punch a few keys, press on the "number lock." Nothing.

"I'm afraid to reboot. I'll lose everything."

Daniel and I have spent every night of the last week until one or two in the morning working on the privilege log. If Jackie has lost it, one or both of us may kill *her*.

"It's not my fault," says Jackie. "This damn document's too big. Too many graphics."

He's hard to miss: six foot five, completely bald, his body like one long muscle. He's an actor; because the lead in *The King and I* has already been filled, however, he earns a living by moonlighting as a word processor.

As with so many facets of life at C & C, there's a protocol when your computer does not work properly or you have to requisition a word processor. Reports must be made; forms must be filled out. Mary is involved.

Jackie ignores them.

When Sam arrives he gives Jackie a giant hug. He's nearly two feet taller than she, but he makes the hug look graceful and natural, as if they weren't members of entirely different species.

"Oh, Sam," coos Jackie, "give me some."

Sam bends down, the patient uncle, and Jackie rubs her hand over his cue-ball head. "It's so smooth," she says to me. "Feel it."

I politely decline. I imagine the picture we would make for any wandering partner.

Jackie explains the problem, how I've "fucked up" her computer with a 100-page chart. Sam listens carefully; he's used to attorneys making unreasonable requests. At three A.M., he's seen the worst.

"Shut it off," he commands.

Both Jackie and I take a step backward, as if Sam had just threatened to hit us. Perhaps this is one time he has met his match.

"Sam—" I begin.

"Just shut it off," he says easily. "It'll save a backup. You can open it when you reboot."

I look to Jackie. She looks back at me and raises her pencil eyebrows. If anyone is going to shut the computer off, I know it's me. Jackie doesn't want any part of the blame. Sam isn't even on the permanent payroll.

I sigh, then walk around behind Jackie's station and flip the switch that controls her computer and printer. It feels like an electrocution. There's a certain pleasure in flipping the switch, diving into the unknown, tossing away my legal career on the whim of a six-foot-five bald guy.

After a minute, Sam instructs me to turn the computer on. We wait as it warms up, races through its system check, brings the familiar icons back onto the screen. Then he tells me to open the word-processing program. I do, and sure enough, a message appears on the screen telling me that a backup version of my document exists, do I want to save it? Of course I do!

I follow Sam's instructions until the chart, my beautiful chart, is back on the screen.

"Now let's see . . . ," says Sam as he sits himself in Jackie's seat.

The document is too big, he tells us; he'll have to chop it up into bite-sized pieces. And while he's at it, who made these lines so thick and uneven, and this column so much larger than that column? He clucks and tuts and clicks his way through the document.

Jackie winks at me and backs away slowly from her secretarial station. The master is at work; do not disturb. Keep hands clear of moving parts.

We had little chance of winning the "common interest" argument. While, in theory, a common interest can exist among a lawyer, his client, and third parties—for example, co-defendants in a criminal prosecution—if investment bankers could keep their business advice confidential in a subsequent lawsuit simply because they shared it with their client's lawyers, legitimate cases of fraud would be much more difficult to prove. All traces of fraudulent activity could be covered by sharing it with lawyers. The attorney-client privilege would become the means to treachery.

The rules of civil procedure and professional ethics require that a lawyer have a reasonable basis for every argument he makes. He can be sanctioned, or wor...

... Charlie could not have known for certain we would lose the privilege argument, just as they didn't know for certain that we would lose the fraud-on-the-market argument that we made on our motion to dismiss. They may have suspected we would lose; they may have assigned a less than twenty percent chance of success; but they still believed there was a possibility of success. They were not so cynical and money-grubbing as to make whatever argument struck their fancy, ethics be damned. In fact, they probably believed that their arguments had real merit. They certainly convinced the client. I sat in Eric's office one afternoon and listened to a conference call in which he recommended to TriCom's board of directors that they withhold documents based on the attorney-client privilege. The directors, none of whom were lawyers, all of whom knew that the insurance company would pay for any action they approved, voted unanimously to go with Eric's recommendation.

The possibility of success was low, Eric admitted. But even if it were only ten percent, the potential payoff was so great that we should take the risk. Denying these documents to the plaintiffs would effectively cripple their case. We also gained a psychological advantage, even if we lost, in that the plaintiffs would know they couldn't expect us to roll over every time they made a demand. This would have a positive effect later on when we began to talk about settlement. Our calculations played to the client's strategy as well: it didn't want to appear to be an easy mark, a defendant that would capitulate whenever the pressure was increased. It would do anything to win.

Eric, of course, had no incentive not to do the work: more work, more money. The client, for its part, would grasp at every possible straw, no matter how thin, because it was not paying the bills. The insurance company had a legal obligation to defend the client, i.e., pay for the client's defense. If it chose not to foot the bill, it could be sued for failing to act in "good faith." What better indicia of bad faith than the fact the insurance company refused to do what the law firm it hired recommended? Unless withholding the documents was one hundred percent meritless, which it was not, the insurance company would lose that lawsuit. In short, nothing could stop Eric from withholding the documents.

In a different world, a lawyer would conduct triage, setting aside the recoverable from the lost causes. This is what lawyers with limited resources, like solo practitioners, do. They do not have a spare army of associates, ready to suit up at a moment's notice. Every extra hour comes right out of their pocket. At a big firm, however, associates are like seats on an airplane; they have value only if they're occupied. If they sit in their office reading *The Wall Street Journal*, they draw the same salary as if they were sitting in the library reading the *Federal Reporter*. Give them something to do, anything; make them bill!

Every new case was a piece of raw meat, and we were hungry dogs. Or so Eric was fond of saying. Litigation is war, was another one of his favorites. Why march ten soldiers into battle if you have one hundred? Why count casualties if you have an endless supply of replacements? Who will stop it? Not the insurance man, with his fear of lawsuits, cozy relationships, and Eric's recommendation. Not the in-house lawyer, with his fear of failure and a zealous boss. The bills are outrageous. The lawyers charge too much. But consider the alternative: no one has ever retained a lawyer who charged too little.

Imagine: you're the General Counsel of a Very Big Corporation that has just been sued by an Extremely Nasty Competitor for Unimaginable Injuries. At stake, the life of the corporation, or at least a significant limb, or at least it feels that way because every lawsuit filed against you threatens to disrupt normal operations. You can hire Joe & Bill's law firm. Two smart guys. Harvard graduates. Their

General Counsel, know all about C & C; in fact, you may have been an associate at C & C, or at a firm just like it. You know that once the shooting starts, it will never stop. You'll send out a document request and get back thirty pages of objections and a privilege log that's larger than the number of documents produced. You'll try to take a deposition and you'll face a motion for a protective order. Every step you take, Eric will be thwacking at your face with a motion, a memo, a brief. He won't stop until he's killed you. Joe and Bill are nice guys, smart guys, hard workers. But it's two of them against the hordes, and while David and Goliath is a nice story, tell it to the beleaguered CEO who thinks he's being outgunned.

Now, make your decision: Joe & Bill's, or C & C?

Nine P.M. The wreckage of dinner strewn across the conference room. Barbecued chicken. Indian food. Burritos. Elizabeth lingers over a diet Coke. Daniel shovels a piece of chocolate cake into his mouth. A few other associates pick through leftovers. The dinner hour has been extended. When I run to the office I sometimes arrive at seven in the morning, though I don't begin working until eight or eight-thirty, but if I leave at seven, I have joined the queue of associates looking for other jobs. No one notices the early risers. Better to keep Daniel's hours of eleven to eleven. Better to linger

over dinner, chatting with my fellows, gossiping about cases, partners, co-workers, than to rush back to my office. What's the hurry?
Do I have a date, a wife, a life?

Julia had asked what I would give to become a partner. Would
you chop off your pinky? she wondered. Just the pinky. Put it on a
cutting board and take a quick cleaver to it. How much could it
hurt? And then you'd be a partner. A partner with nine fingers, I
said. Yeah, but a partner; and who needs a pinky?

But no one's offered, even if it were that simple. Instead, I am slog-
ging through the usual route: memos and briefs, document production and discovery. I have all my fingers, though my eyes are failing.

The other associates at the table all have their pinkies on the table.
Partners are wielding hatchets, tomahawks, and worse. Entire limbs
are missing. One woman has cut short her honeymoon in St. Bart's
to work on a temporary restraining order. Another more senior associate has canceled a vacation he rescheduled after canceling once
before this year. His wife and daughter, losing patience, have gone
to Europe without him. A third claims he has not set foot in his
apartment for two weeks. We share these stories like baseball cards:
buy 'em, swap 'em, collect 'em. Tales, not of misery, but of valor.
Because even as the woman recounts the phone call to her honeymoon hotel room, her face illumines with pride. *They said they
needed me.* In boot camp, you learn to love the officers.

There's a certain shared esteem in being an associate at this table.
And despite the fact that I don't really like any of these associates,
I feel a kinship with them. On one level we are competitors for the
prize that will elude most of us: partnership. But we also know that
the chances of becoming partner are so slim as to be nonexistent;
thus, we really have no reason to compete. We also share a common
enemy: the partners who have made us stay late in this conference
room, eating dinner with each other when we really should be home
with loved ones. These are the moments when it is never clearer who
are the employees and who the owners. *We* are in the conference
room; the partners are not.

But all good things must end. Daniel licks the remnants of chocolate from his fingers. I drain my watery soda. We bid good night, or is it good morning, to our peers, and return to our own airtight conference room.

Date/Author/Recipient(s)/Type/Description/Privilege

ument seems unremarkable to me.

"What's the privilege?" I ask Daniel, waving a page scrawled with a client's handwritten notes. We've done this before.

"It's the client asking lawyers for advice."

"What advice?"

"Do I need to disclose this information for the stock offering?" he says. "The fact Tricom's lawyers asked for it reflects their legal opinion that the information has to be disclosed."

That's the argument, but it feels half-baked even as he says it. I know that Eric has ordained that these documents are privileged, and I know that he believes it. But how much "good faith" does a lawyer need to make a good-faith argument? I wonder. If he can make it without laughing, is that enough? Lawyers are trained to construct arguments from the flimsiest cloth; a good lawyer could argue convincingly that the sun rises at night, sets in the east, influences the tides. What is night; what is east; have you ever seen gravity?

I carry several penciled pages of the privilege log to Sam. He is typing away happily on Jackie's computer. No music, no distractions, just him and the graphical beauty of WordPerfect for Windows. He acknowledges me with a slight dip of his bald crown as he slips my pages to the bottom of his pile.

When I return to the conference room, Daniel has borrowed the boom box and a stack of CDs from the associate down the hall. A raucous tune blasts from its grilles as if from a loaded Camaro on a Saturday night.

"What is this?" I ask.

"Music," he says.

"Are you sure?"

He doesn't take the bait. Instead, the edges of his mouth curl away from the plane of his face. It's one of the few times I've seen him smile, and I can't say it's unattractive. In fact, it's a little bit like looking out on a neglected garden and discovering that what seemed like weeds have bloomed into flowers. I suddenly see him as Abby might, and he's almost handsome.

I don't mind the noise. The rhythmic chants, the chirping guitars, the crunching drums. It's a postmodern lullaby, and it soon works its magic. I read through the documents in a half-trance of sleep, barely awake to mark the pages for privilege.

Two A.M. Waiting for a cab. Taxis cruise up Park Avenue, their off-duty lights like taunts. There must be a strike, or a change in shifts, or maybe they're making their escape from New York.

A Lincoln slows, honks. At this hour there are only perils: drug dealer, drug buyer, prostitute, tourist. He honks again and I look up. Sam waves to me from the rear window. "Need a ride?" he asks.

Trust Sam to do the smart thing, to call for a car in the wee hours instead of trying to save the client a few dollars. I climb aboard.

"You live on the West Side," he says.

I wonder how he knows. Has he been following me?

"I see you sometimes on the subway," he explains.

I'm suddenly embarrassed that Sam has spotted me but I've never seen him, as if I've exposed myself as the elitist I fear I am. My radar doesn't register below a certain altitude in the firm hierarchy. Yet how could I miss a six-foot-five bald man?

"I can't make conversation in the morning," he apologizes. "I barely remember my lines."

I realize he's embarrassed for not acknowledging me. At that hour he's probably in another world—an actor, not a word processor. Greeting a lawyer is a kiss of death, certain to ostracize him off-Broadway.

"Are you in something?" I ask.

"I'm not gay," he adds, in case I was worried.

The driver's radio comes to life with a staccato burst of language, maybe Dutch. The driver, however, speaks Russian, loudly. There's a barrage of miscommunication until Sam asks him to turn the radio down. The driver frowns, but complies. I envy Sam his ability to issue commands. I can barely ask Jackie to make copies.

"So are you doing anything else besides our chart?" Sam turns back to me.

"I'm playing the lawyer in a long-running farce," I say.

"A case of mistaken identity," he offers.

"Thank you," I say, though I'm not sure he means it as a compliment.

"You're not the lawyer type," he continues.

Is he sure he's been spying on the right person?

"You should see these guys, the way they freak out—as if the world awaits their redlining. They think we're idiots. And the women are worse. I don't know how you work with them."

I feel myself bristling with self-defensiveness, as if he has insulted my family. It's all right to call your own mother a jerk, but if someone else does, *them's* fighting words.

"They're not so bad," I say. "They're just overworked."

"That woman, Caroline, she screamed at me for right-justifying her document. And she's not even a partner." Sam looks out the window. "I always right-justify," he adds sadly.

Poor Sam. Everywhere he turns he's confronted by the computer-illiterate. He only wants to punch the clock, do his job, go home to his life. Instead, lawyers compromise his aesthetic sensibilities by forcing him to reduce to ragged edges the right margins of their motions.

"There's a lot of anal retentiveness," I offer.

"I'm as anal as the next guy," he admits. "I'm talking about civility. You don't see it, because you're a lawyer, but most of your bosses treat us like shit, and worse."

I know what he means. The dinner hour buzzes with stories of partners who mistreat support staff. Stanley Cohen, Barry Katz's mentor, has gone through five secretaries since my first day. You can hear him all the way at the end of the hallway on the thirty-fifth floor yelling about this misplaced document, that misfiled correspondence. Every secretary was a fool; every messenger a dolt. But at least he doesn't play favorites: he once threw a book at Barry for missing a case citation in a memorandum.

"The associates aren't like that," I say.

"You'll see," Sam says sagely. "They change."

"I won't."

"You will, or you'll leave. It's self-selection," he explains. "Only the cruelest survive."

Sam's evaluation seems unduly harsh. There are tyrants among the partners, though no one's thrown anything at me, and I've noticed how senior associates seem to share the traits of their mentors, the way husbands and wives often look like each other and people look like their dogs or their cars. I doubt Barry began work at C & C by calling his secretary a "dope," but after watching Stanley's behavior, he changed. Yet most C & C attorneys are decent souls, their worst traits explained by overwork and a battlefield mentality. They expect everyone to join them in the trenches even when, like Sam, the staff hasn't enlisted for combat.

"Then why do you stay?" I ask.

"I've been here a long time. I don't let that stuff get to me. Besides, where am I going to go? It's not like another firm is any better. And Broadway is dead, in case you haven't heard."

Sam is about thirty-five, I would guess. He wears a barely visible veneer of bronze makeup

from the sky

they barely make a splash when they land.

The car slows on my block. Sam asks my address and directs the driver to the correct apartment. When he tries to stop at the corner, Sam insists he drive the extra half-block to my door. The driver knows enough not to argue.

"You have a voucher?" I ask.

Sam looks at me as if I've asked if he is wearing pants. He's been signing vouchers since my parents were signing my report cards. He waves me off with the back of his hand.

"You going to need me tomorrow?" he asks. In the word-processing pool, he takes whatever stray appears on his doorstep. He doesn't have a choice.

"Are you free?"

"I'm always free."

"See you tomorrow, then."

Sam nods, and the car drives off. I am left feeling a strange mixture of guilt and pleasure. Guilt at giving him work, pleasure because I can.

Weekends like weekdays. Saturday a casual version of Monday. I wear jeans and a T-shirt to the office, order pizza, prop my feet on the library tables. Other associates stop to chat, share a slice, exchange office gossip. The taboo against food and speech in a library is not easily broken; we keep our voices low and pizza hidden despite the absence of the librarian. Occasionally, a partner or senior associate strolls along the hallway outside the library in his pressed khakis and button-down shirt. He says hello, asks what we are working on, feigns interest in our research projects. If we sit near the window, across the room, they never stop.

This Saturday, as I leave her apartment, Kate offers to come with me.

"That's no fun," I protest. In truth, I can't imagine bringing my girlfriend to the office. No one does, at least as far as I know, though sometimes a husband or wife will arrive to pick up their spouse and linger for a minute or two. It's always a shock to realize a colleague has a life outside the office, more corporeal than the two-dimensional photo on the desk.

"I went to those summer things."

Shakespeare in the Park is not the same as Saturday in the library, I explain.

"Pretty much," she says.

"I thought you liked the play."

"The play's okay," rhymes Kate. "It's the company I could miss."

"It's still the same company."

"That's why you need me."

"I do," I say. "Believe me. This is for your sake."

It's bad enough that office life bleeds into home life. But once people bring their homes into the office, I think, the ramparts have been breached and the castle violated. There is no longer a castle.

"We could shoot spitballs at the partners."

"They won't be there," I say.

"Why not?"

"They have their work sent home." I explain how associates copy, highlight, and arrange in neat binders all the relevant case law, statutes, memoranda, and other documents that a partner could possibly desire to review over the weekend in the comfort and security of their own doorman apartments or vacation homes.

"That's the life," says Kate. "How do you get one of those jobs?"

"They still have to work," I say, growing a little perturbed with Kate's efforts to secure me alternative employment.

"They're not working if they're doing it in the Hamptons."

"Please," I say.

"Is Elizabeth Jewish?" Kate asks.

"No, but that's not the point. The partner is."

"Maybe he didn't want to celebrate Passover. Maybe that was exactly the excuse he needed."

I'm about to protest, to let my annoyance with Kate loose. She's playing devil's advocate when I need a guardian angel. But I realize, as I prepare to complain, that she may be right. The partners with the cell phones, do they really need to be reached anywhere? Or is their desire for constant communication about feeling important while avoiding the awkward obligations of family life? Their children act up, their spouses grow silent, the Jewish holidays oppress them. Why bother? They closet themselves in their study with fax machine, laptop, and document binders. Through work comes their freedom.

"Is that why you've always got a manuscript when I come over?" I ask instead.

"Me? Who's going to work?"

"I don't have a choice."

"Stay home and I'll give you one."

"Kat."

"Stay."

So I do. And she does.

*   *   *

The hearing before the magistrate was scheduled for a Friday afternoon. Eric decided that someone who actually prepared the privilege
log should attend. Because Daniel was in depositions with Jensen,
and Eric himself out of town on another case, Charlie and I took a
car for another ride down to Centre Street and the magistrate's
chambers.

Charlie had prepared the Memorandum in Opposition to Plaintiff's Motion to Compel the Production of Privileged Documents by
himself. Perhaps he felt Daniel and I had done such a poor job on
the last memorandum we wrote that he wasn't going to bestow on
us a second chance. Or maybe he was tired of going through the
motions of appearing to give associates an opportunity to do substantive work. It was simpler, easier, faster for him to write the memo
directly, without the muddle of our brains. Eric said it was because
Daniel and I were occupied with the privilege log.

"You ready?" I ask in the car, to say something, anything, in the
oppressive silence.

"For what?" he asks.

To get your ass kicked, I feel like saying. Instead, I say, "For the
argument."

"The magistrate's made up his mind. He's giving them the documents." A stubble of blood, razor burn, fans across Charlie's jowls.

Why are we here, then? I wonder again. Why have I spent every
night for the last three weeks working past midnight on the privilege log?

As if he's heard my thoughts, or perhaps seen the lost expression
on my face, Charlie adds, "You never know. Maybe we'll get lucky."

Luck, I think, has nothing to do with it. A lawyer reads the cases,
analogizes them to his facts, and estimates the chances of success.
Guessing incorrectly is not the same thing as bad luck. And guessing
correctly that you'll lose is another matter entirely.

Charlie doesn't say anything more, and I'm content to watch the
architecture as we weave and lurch through lower Manhattan. Each
wave of immigrants has claimed part of this city as its own, only

to be replaced by the next wave. And here I am, being driven in a Lincoln Town Car through the streets my grandparents fled, wearing a $1,000 suit, billing my time at $180 an hour.

The driver deposits us at the federal courthouse on Foley Square amid the hulking regime of government buildings. While the state

state court judge. The hushed and unmarred walls a stark contrast to the screaming proceedings in state court. Even the doorknobs shine.

Charlie signs us in, and we sit on a gleaming wooden pew near the rear of the courtroom. Two lawyers for the plaintiffs, whom I have not seen before, wait on the other side of the room. They do not look at us.

After several minutes, the magistrate's law clerk enters the courtroom and calls us back to the magistrate's chambers. I had expected a more formal argument, with the magistrate assuming the bench, and each side standing before him as Eric had done with our motion for summary judgment, and as every law student does in Moot Court. *May it please the Court*, we begin.

"This is an enormous number of documents," the magistrate says gravely when we are seated in his chambers, before we've had a minute to introduce ourselves or state our positions. He holds up the privilege log, grown to 258 pages. "And quite an imposing chart."

I can't help my smile. *An imposing chart. An awe-inspiring chart. A chart without equal.* I quickly force the corners of my mouth into a frown. I don't want anyone to think I don't take these proceedings seriously.

The magistrate continues talking, but I have lost my way. I am enthralled to be in his chambers, so close to the next best thing to an Article III judge. I am a lawyer; I practice law. If I said something, he might even listen. Charlie is speaking, and I mentally urge him to direct a question to me. But a lawyer for the plaintiffs cuts him off, and the conversation veers in a different direction.

"I don't see how this is any different than any other securities offering," the magistrate says. "If I sustained the privilege wouldn't that insulate the entire drafting process from scrutiny?"

"The issuer shares a common interest with the underwriter," Charlie says. "It's no different than the issuer communicating with its own attorney."

"And with counsel to the underwriter? And with its PR firm? And with its accountants? There're dozens of third parties here," plaintiffs' lawyer jumps in.

"That's my problem," says the magistrate. "Haven't you waived the privilege by disclosing to third parties?"

"Not to third parties with whom the issuer shares a common interest," says Charlie.

"Well, now we're just going around in circles," says the magistrate.

Charlie's face, I notice, is a patchwork of red and white blotches, a psoriatic quilt. I worry that he might erupt.

The plaintiffs' lawyer cites a string of cases, and Charlie cites another string. The magistrate follows the Ping-Pong of conversation with rapidly dwindling interest. I sneak a peek at his clerk; she is chewing at the end of a nail. Clearly, a decision has been made, probably before we even entered the room. Why are we wasting their time?

Finally, the magistrate says, "I haven't looked at every document in this chart." He holds my chart again as if it were something sacred. "But I'm going order defendant to produce documents that have been shared with third parties. If you want to revise the chart and withhold documents that have been shared only with your client's attorneys, I'll consider another privilege argument. But I have to tell you, it better be privileged. I don't want to look at another three-hundred-page monstrosity."

A *monstrosity*? I feel the weight of my privilege log crumple around my shoulders. I thought I had created a work of beauty, a billable piece of art, only to discover I am Dr. Frankenstein

..., neither, apparently, has Charlie. It comes with the job description.

A cold wind sweeps across the plaza as we step from the car. We hurry back into the office. The elevator whisks us silently upstairs.

"How'd it go?" asks Jackie when she sees me coming down the corridor.

I don't respond.

"That bad," she says, then asks, "Want a Life Saver?"

Count on Jackie to crack a joke when I could really use one.

"That was my entire summer and most of my fall," I whine.

"That's what I said about my ex-husband," says Jackie.

"I thought you were married for six years."

"I said it every fall."

She wins. I smile.

"It's just a job," she reminds me. "Did you do your best?"

"You saw the chart."

"It was one hell of a chart," Jackie agrees.

We both are quiet for a moment, nodding in fond recollection at the sheer prodigiousness of the privilege log. Then I shake my head and shuffle toward my office.

"Hey," calls Jackie, stopping me. She tears the wrapping paper off a roll and places a hard, round, sweet candy in my palm.

I suck on it.

On the Road (Again)

My new case materialized, emerging from the depths of Eric's office like a forgotten cousin, now heralded. It was a simple breach of contract action between a supplier of road salt and one of its customers. Normally, it was not the kind of case C & C would take; there was not a lot of money involved, and there were no complicated issues of law. In fact, it made no sense for the company to hire an expensive firm like C & C when there were perfectly competent and less expensive alternatives. The client, however, was the subsidiary of a much larger construction conglomerate for which C & C was trying to do more work. Thus, C & C had an incentive to keep its bills down to entice the corporate parent's work, while the corporate parent could get a good look at C & C before plunging into a long-term and expensive relationship.

Our new client, Diamond Gravel, had a contract with its customer, a company called Target Sand & Stone, in which Target promised to buy a certain amount of road salt from Diamond during the year. The dispute centered on the amount of salt Target was obligated to purchase. Diamond claimed that the contract language required Target to buy a minimum of approximately $750,000 worth of salt, whether or not Target needed it. Target claimed the $750,000 figure was an estimate, based on its needs from previous winters. The dispute arose following a warm winter with little snow and little need for deicing. Target had purchased only $150,000 worth of salt, for which it had paid in full. Diamond claimed it was owed $600,000 on the original contract. Target disagreed.

the contract language, which the court held was ambiguous. Best of all, she promised, we would share in the preparation, and I would have the opportunity to examine witnesses—my own witnesses—on the stand.

Maybe, I thought, I did work well with Caroline, after all.

Suddenly, I had three active cases: Dekor Industries, TriCom, and Diamond Gravel. While three cases might seem laughable to a public defender or a personal injury lawyer who handled scores of cases at one time, it was a heavy burden for a young associate at C & C. Daniel had two cases, and on one of them, TriCom, I was doing at least half the work. Jay had worked on one case for almost the entire last year. To have few cases was a luxury; it was also a tremendous burden.

Associates took the work as it was dished out to them. Partners rarely kept us in the decision-making loop. Work appeared without warning, landing on one's desk in the form of a pile of documents, or a pink message slip, ruining the week, or the weekend, or both. We had no control over when depositions would be scheduled, when document requests were due; these decisions were made by partners or senior associates who consulted their own calendars and informed us as an afterthought. Each partner assumed his case was our only one, or at least they all acted that way. Thus, the burden of multiple cases arose from our inability to control the flow of work and the singular expectations of partners and senior associates.

So, of course, just as I was gearing up on Diamond Gravel, both Dekor and TriCom reared their ugly heads.

First, Charlie had scheduled depositions in Detroit in the Dekor case. Not to be outgunned, the plaintiffs had scheduled their own depositions. The scheduling involved delicate maneuverings among lawyers, clients, and deponents. Some deponents had their own lawyers, others were represented by plaintiff's counsel or by C & C; some were clients, others merely witnesses. By the time Charlie presented me with the schedule, he had been negotiating dates for weeks among the various parties; he did not ask about my calendar.

Then Eric informed me he had arranged for me to travel to Boston to collect documents in response to a second document request in the TriCom case. Daniel would be occupied by Jensen, and was not available. Eric knew about the depositions in Detroit, but told me the sooner I could get to Boston, the better. Perhaps I could arrange a trip between depositions. This was physically impossible, unless I worked in Detroit during the day and Boston at night, but when I told Eric he said simply, "Do the best you can."

With all the commotion, Diamond Gravel slipped to third on a list of three. Caroline didn't protest, however, and neither did I. She seemed to be content knowing that I was assigned to her case. Once there, her urgency for my presence disappeared as if it were never needed in the first place. Perhaps it wasn't.

Detroit, my second home.

We have traveled here again, with a cargo of documents, a computerized database, a paralegal, and a pile of deposition scripts, as if filming a bad television movie. I don't know when I'll return.

There are twelve depositions scheduled, eight for them, four for us, with others to be arranged shortly. We have round-trip tickets, but without a return date. We have open-ended hotel reservations.

We have two rental cars, in case our tasks take us in opposite directions. We have everything an attorney might need for an indefinite stay in America's heartland.

"Don't forget to write," said Kate as I carried two bulging litigation briefcases and a suitcase from her apartment. She peered over *The New York Times* ...

... Consolidated trial, created a database of documents collected and produced in the case. With a simple search term, he was able to retrieve all the relevant documents.

Based on the documents, and on what was alleged in the complaint and from the meager facts we had learned from Hamilton Williams, Dekor's general counsel, I outlined areas of deposition preparation for our witnesses. Our primary goal, in defending the witnesses' depositions, was to keep their stories on our side of the fence. There were only three or four documents that suggested Dekor had engaged in price-fixing, but those could be explained as the efforts of a savvy marketer to keep a close watch on its competition and to match them price for price. At least that was our theme. For each witness we defended I summarized, at Charlie's instruction and to the extent the information was available, his name, background, work experience, job responsibilities, place in the Dekor hierarchy, and possible topics of examination. I spent a lot of time on the phone with Hamilton Williams's assistant, Carrie, whose knowledge of everyone's place in the company was unsurpassed. She complained that the lawsuit swallowed all her time, but she was unfailingly cheerful and helpful, and I suspected that she welcomed the diversion.

Because we were taking, as well as defending, depositions, I wrote a set of deposition questions that, Charlie being Charlie, he immediately revised until it bore no resemblance to the original. My questions were broad and brief, similar to the outlines I prepared for our witnesses. I tried to cover all the documents received by the witness and all areas in which the witness had any knowledge. Charlie's revisions were specific and lengthy. When I wrote, "Background questions," Charlie wrote, "State your name," "State your address," "State your age," "State your occupation," and so on. In truth, I didn't really know exactly what "background questions," were, but I assumed Charlie would. Still, I was shocked to see a man who had taken scores of depositions require every question written out like a schoolboy's first exam.

Now Charlie and I sit in one of the cavernous conference rooms somewhere near Hamilton Williams's office with a man named Frank Paterno. Wilson is in another room organizing documents for the next prep session with a different witness. Frank has authored one of the "problematic" documents, a memorandum that indicates Dekor Industries had met with a competitor and agreed to "formalize bidding structures."

A lawyer cannot tell his client to lie, or sit quietly if he does. But a lawyer can shape and mold and revise and cajole a witness into the party line. Charlie doesn't ask Frank what he meant when he wrote "formalize bidding structures." Instead, Charlie tells Frank what Steven Kormac, another Dekor witness and Frank's supervisor, told us about this meeting with the competitor. According to Charlie, according to Kormac, the purpose of the meeting was to discuss a possible merger. Frank doesn't remember this discussion.

"Why would we merge with them?" he asks.

"Is Kormac your supervisor?" asks Charlie.

"Sure."

"Does Kormac tell you everything about his business plans?"

"Not everything."

"Ever been to a meeting with Kormac where you later learned the meeting had a different purpose or you didn't know the purpose?"

"Sure, I guess."

"Kormac told us that after the meeting the parties decided not to further their merger discussion."

"He did?"

"There was going to be a formal bid, but the bankers could never reach agreement on the structure."

"That's fine," says Charlie. "If you have no specific recollection we don't want you speculating or guessing what you meant. If you're asked about this document you can simply say 'I don't know' or 'I can't remember.' Everything you testify to has to be from your personal knowledge. If you don't remember exactly what you meant, don't guess."

"Okay," says Frank.

Next witness.

Monday morning. One week after our arrival. Seven billable days at twelve billable hours a day. The cavernous conference room is now populated by Charlie, me, our local counsel, Wilson, Hamilton Williams, two lawyers for the plaintiff, their paralegal, an attorney from the Justice Department who is investigating criminal charges against Dekor, a video operator, a court reporter, and, nearly forgotten among the clutter, the first witness, Frank Paterno. Secretaries come and go with documents, faxes, notes, telephone messages, coffee, iced water, soda, sandwiches, cookies. Though our group is large, the conference room is still larger, a professional football stadium occupied by the Sunday morning pickup game.

An electric current charges the room, or is it me? The other participants, except for Frank, appear bored. They've done this drill before. But for me this is practically like being at trial. There's no judge, and no jury, but there are two advocates locked in combat, about to embark on a grueling regime of questioning, answering, objecting, and truth seeking. These are the moments I've been waiting for, of which there have been too few so far. The opportunity to get to the heart of the matter, to peel back the layers of procedure and posturing to reach the merits within. And even though it's not me who's doing the peeling, it's as close as I've come.

"Do you swear to tell the truth the whole truth and nothing but the truth?" intones the court reporter.

"Sure," says Frank.

"Please state your name for the record," begins the plaintiff's lead attorney.

"Frank Paterno."

"Could you spell that?"

"F-R-A-N-K."

"Your last name, please."

"P-A-T-E-R-N-O."

"What is your home address?"

"One-oh-seven Sycamore Drive, Southfield, Michigan."

"Mr. Paterno, could you please describe your educational background, beginning with the high school you attended?

"Mr. Paterno, could you please describe the first job you had upon your graduation from college?

"What were your responsibilities in that position?

"How many employees did you supervise?

"To whom did you report?

"How long did you stay in that position?

"What were your reasons for departing?

"And what was the next job you obtained?"

The morning passes in an increasingly numbing haze of seemingly irrelevant questions. I keep waiting for the fireworks, but by the lunch break we have barely covered Frank's educational background and work experience.

"Who's paying for this?" asks Hamilton Williams when we retreat to his office. He should know; he's not a litigator, but he is an attorney. Yet he's suddenly cost-conscious after months of chatting our ears off with impunity.

"You are," says Charlie.

"Can't they speed it up?"

Charlie shrugs. When his turn comes, he knows he will be equally

Frank's educational background and work history. I'm just making conversation, giving Charlie the bat to knock the lawyers out of the park for their verbosity, but instead he takes me seriously and says that learning a witness's education and history is important because the witness may have some specialized training to call upon at trial, or may lack any qualifications and can be impeached on that basis.

Who am I to disagree? Never mind that Frank is a fact witness, with no expert qualifications in anything, that the sole purpose for his deposition is to explain what he meant when he wrote "formalize bidding structures," that as far as I can see his deposition should take exactly twenty minutes. It would still leave plenty of time for the relevant background questions.

But no associate wants to return to the office after a twenty-minute deposition and call it complete, just as no associate wants to leave at six o'clock and call it a day. What would the partners think? And there is no reason to keep the deposition short. The associate won't go home any earlier; he won't impress the client, his peers, or bosses; in fact, if he takes a short deposition he will reduce his billable hours and call his thoroughness into question. So he asks another question.

After lunch, we move into more substantive areas: organizational structure, management hierarchy, workplace definition. It is not until close to four o'clock that we finally tackle the memo.

"Directing your attention to Paterno exhibit eighteen," says the plaintiff's attorney. "Is that your signature at the bottom of the first page?"

"Sure," says Frank.

"Do you recognize this document?"

"Sure. I wrote it."

"What is this document?"

"Objection," says Charlie. "The document speaks for itself."

"You can answer," says the plaintiff's attorney to Frank.

Frank looks at Charlie, who says, "The record will reflect that Paterno eighteen is a memo from Frank Paterno to Stanley Joseph re: May 16 meeting."

The plaintiff's attorney gives Charlie a sour look. What Charlie has done, strictly speaking, is against the rules that prohibit coaching witnesses during a deposition. In essence, Charlie has told Frank how to answer the question. On the other hand, Charlie can claim innocence because he has simply identified the document for the record, something the plaintiff's attorney should have done before asking Frank about it.

"It's a memo I wrote to Mr. Joseph after a May sixteenth meeting with your client," says Frank.

The plaintiff's attorney frowns, but lets his annoyance with Charlie go unrecorded.

"What was the purpose of the memo?"

"To summarize for Mr. Joseph what went on at the meeting."

"Directing your attention to the handwriting along the side of the exhibit. Do you recognize the handwriting?"

"It's mine."

"Will you read it out loud, please?"

" 'Formalize bidding structures.' "

"What did you mean when you wrote 'formalize bidding structures'?"

"I don't know."

"You don't know?"

"I don't remember."

"You don't remember?"

"No," says Frank.

"No, you do, or no, you don't?" the lawyer asks.

"No, I don't," says Frank.

"This is your handwriting, correct?"

"Correct."

"You wrote this?"

⟨text obscured⟩

I'm not sure what I meant."

"Didn't you write this memo?"

"Objection, asked and answered. Badgering the witness."

"It was four years ago. I can't remember exactly. I don't want to guess."

"No, don't guess," says the plaintiff's attorney caustically. "None of us want you to guess."

"Then that's all I have to say."

The plaintiff's attorney asks a few more perfunctory questions, but it's clear the deposition has ended. It has taken six hours to ask a two-minute series of questions that have elicited exactly zero. We have faced the enemy and he is ours, defeated by the rules of evidence and the foibles of human memory. Sometimes you have to be prepared to forget.

If it's Wednesday, this must be Boston.

I've returned to New York for one day, long enough to wash my underwear, pick up my shirts at the dry cleaner's, see Kate for dinner, then pack for my next trip. We ran out of time in Detroit, schedules unraveled, witnesses became unavailable, attorneys had other emergencies. We completed only five depositions, three of theirs, two of ours. Threats were made to reconvene into the following weeks, but no one was actually available. In any event, the

TriCom document production had taken on an urgent note. The TriCom plaintiffs were threatening motions, sanctions, conferences with the magistrate. Eric ordered me to return for battle.

Now the Boston shuttle fills like a game of leapfrog. Middle seats remain empty, storage counters for suit jackets and extra papers, while windows and aisles are quickly occupied. I sit at the window. The woman in the aisle seat works on a laptop computer while talking on the airphone. If she were any more wireless, she would be floating.

Practically before we take off, we've landed. I rent a car and drive to Route 128, Boston's Silicon Valley. I'm already an old hand at airports, car rentals, hotels, homes away from home. I feel like a lawyer, or a traveling salesman, my briefcase filled with wares. I'm entirely on my own for the very first time, without introduction or accompaniment by Charlie, and I almost believe I know what I'm doing.

TriCom's corporate headquarters is a relatively small building in an office park, a smaller sibling to Dekor Industries' bronze mono-lith. TRICOM—LEADERSHIP THROUGH TECHNOLOGY, the sign on the perfectly manicured lawn announces. Beyond the edges of the lawn, the grass degrades into dirt, broken concrete, and weeds. I park the car in an empty visitors' lot and lock the door.

There's no receptionist when I arrive. I stand awkwardly by the reception desk waiting for someone to admit or announce me. The reception area opens onto a large room filled with about a dozen cubicles that are also vacant. Several of the cubicles have computers, and several of the computers are on, but no one seems to be work-ing. The whole place has the feeling of a façade, the unoccupied set for a movie about business. It is not a good omen for a company charged with securities fraud.

Finally, a young woman who looks vaguely Eurasian strolls from a rear office toward the reception area. She seems unconcerned to see me standing there. I could be an industrial spy, the Unabomber, a third-world agitator.

"You must be the lawyer," she says.

The suit was her first clue, my worried expression her second.

I tell her I've come to gather and copy documents in response to a lawsuit. She knows all about me. The chairman is busy right now, she tells me, but he's instructed her to direct me to whatever files I need.

Is there some sort of central file?" I ask.

"There's a central place, yes," she says. "But it is not everything. Many people keep their own correspondence. They do not send it."

"How many people?"

"We had twelve in sales. Now we have ten."

"How many people in the office altogether?"

She thinks, counting on her fingers. "Seventeen," she concludes.

There's probably a better way, and no doubt in a huge corporation there would have to be, but this is the easiest way I can think of.

"I need to see all their files," I decide.

"All?" she repeats.

"Every last one," I say.

I am the lawyer; I decide. And, to my surprise, she obeys.

I spent most of the first day at TriCom getting acquainted with the office. While there were seventeen TriCom employees, three were secretaries and one was the receptionist, whose name was Katja. They didn't have files. Of the ten salespeople, only five had extensive files. The remaining three employees were the chairman of the board and two vice presidents. Only one of the vice presidents kept files. The other two, according to Katja, threw out every piece of paper that crossed their desks.

All that day I never saw more than three people. Everyone else was out of town, Katja told me. Tomorrow, she promised, the chairman would return.

I drove back to my hotel in the suburbs early. I had a book, the first novel I had tried to read in a year. I had a selection of ten movies on pay-per-view. My wish to be alone while traveling had been granted, and suddenly I didn't want it. The sterile hotel room. The empty offices. The airless shuttle ride. I needed some human contact, a kind and familiar face.

While I hadn't spoken with her in months, I knew Abby was at Harvard, enmeshed in her first year of law school. I got her number from information and gave her a call. She answered the phone after one ring. While she sounded surprised to hear from me, she also sounded happy. She had just returned from an informational meeting for students interested in writing for the law review, and her voice sounded high-pitched with stress. At Harvard, as at many other schools, becoming a law review editor was no longer simply a function of grades. If you wanted the golden blessing of law review membership, you had to participate in a weeklong writing competition.

Like most of my first-year classmates, I had picked up the materials for law review when final exams ended. Because half the people were selected based entirely on the writing competition (the other half were selected based on grades and writing), a completely mediocre student like myself could become an editor, an honor formerly bestowed only on those with the highest grade-point average. Law review was one more rung in a life of ladders. After law review came federal court clerkships and then, for the truly gifted, a Supreme Court clerkship.

Law review, we were told by professors and by second- and third-year students, was essential for those who wanted to clerk, and clerking (especially for a federal judge) was essential for those who wanted the best jobs. While a Harvard degree alone could get most of us a job with a firm like C & C, it could not guarantee partnership, a tenure-track faculty position, a judicial nomination, a government appointment, a job with the U.S. Attorney's office. Law review came with no guarantees, but miss it and forgo one more step into the legal firmament.

I hauled my thousand-page law review packet to my parents' summer house in Cape Cod. The assignment was simple, if tedious. Take a poorly written law review article and edit it. Check the citations

house was empty and filled with light. The day held nothing but promise.

I threw the packet in the trash.

I had blown my chance to be anything but a normal Harvard graduate. Yet at the time I felt virtuous; I had resisted the urge to keep clambering heavenward. I did not want to be a law review editor; I saw nothing enjoyable about the opportunity to edit inscrutable manuscripts. And that honest emotion drove me to resist.

The next year, however, I enrolled in the upper-level Moot Court competition because I feared that my résumé was woefully inadequate. One of my teammates was a friend who had not made law review. Moot Court, he explained, was our chance to redeem ourselves. Distinction, at any cost, was worth the grimness of the late nights, the additional burden of researching and writing a thirty-page appellate brief while keeping up with our course work. The skills learned seemed like an afterthought. When we won, after three semesters of competition, I could not remember the person who had thrown the law review packet in the trash.

Now, nearly four years after that June morning, I drove to Cambridge and met Abby at a restaurant near her apartment. As we ate, we discussed law review, and she advanced the standard reasons for participating in the writing competition. She thought it would be a "good experience," and she thought she would "learn a lot." She also hoped to clerk after law school, and law review, she believed, was essential in that quest.

As I listened to Abby, I felt abstracted from the whole process, and critical of her decisions. She seemed to be advancing blindly, transcript in one hand, résumé in the other. All the old emotions I had experienced while sitting in my parents' backyard returned, and I remembered my reasons for throwing out the law review packet. Why did she want to cite-check manuscripts? I pressed her. And why clerk? She would be a glorified research assistant, a judge's lackey. It would be interesting, she claimed, to see the workings of a courtroom from the inside. And why work at a big firm this summer? I continued. The experience, she claimed, and the training. Besides, who was I to question her choices?

She was right, of course. From my perch at C & C it was easy to criticize the choices made by others. What did I expect from her? To join the ACLU? Fight for civil justice reform? I had been at C & C for a year and a half and I hadn't even taken on a case *pro bono*, for no reason other than my own inertia. Instead, every two weeks a large paycheck was deposited in my checking account. It was as if I were two persons: the one who missed law review, and the one who made Moot Court. These two sides of my personality were constantly at war, one driving me up the ladder, the other keeping me grounded. I wasn't arguing with Abby, I was arguing with myself.

In my life I had been rewarded by the smiles and praises of adults for my good grades, my high board scores, my noteworthy extra-curricular activities. I had learned to achieve for this praise. Soon, it became impossible to distill where I began and others ended. Law school, Moot Court, big firm, which would I have pursued if left to my own desires? What were my desires? I didn't know anything about Abby's life; perhaps she truly wanted these things. Perhaps she was right to want them. In a generation of ambivalents, there must still be those with Scott Turow's convictions.

Abby ate quickly, excusing herself to prepare for her Thursday morning classes. I paid the bill, saving the receipt for reimbursement, and we left. As I drove alone back to my hotel, I realized we hadn't talked about anything else but law.

"The chairman is arriving this afternoon," promises Katja.

"Whatever," I say, in my best American accent.

documents vertically in the file or, more often, if the whole file is relevant, I remove the entire drawer and flip the file vertically amid its fellows. I label the outside of the box with the location of the file or files. My plan is to instruct a copy service, one specializing in copying documents for lawyers, to make three copies of the vertical documents or files: a pristine set for our files, a working set, and a set to be turned over to the plaintiffs' lawyers.

The fourth office I visit belongs to a young salesman named David Rosenberg. He reminds me of dozens of kids with whom I went to high school, complete with Long Island accent, curly hair, and hazel eyes. He's reading the paper when I enter his office.

"I got nothing," he says when I explain what I'm looking for.

"No contracts, no correspondence?" I ask, somewhat incredulously.

"Mostly junk," he says, waving at his file cabinet.

"Can I look?"

"Suit yourself," he says. "I don't even know what's in there."

If he doesn't know what's in his files, how does he know he doesn't have any relevant documents? I wonder, but don't ask.

He keeps his feet propped on the desk while I open the top file drawer. The very first label I see says: CONTRACTS. That file is further subdivided by name. The names spill out of the file drawer and down into the next one. When I step back I notice that the entire filing cabinet, comprising four drawers, is divided by letter ranges labeled at the front of each drawer: A–E, F–K, L–R, S–Z.

I scan the first drawer of contract documents. They are contracts between TriCom and various vendors, software and hardware manufacturers.

"I'm going to need to copy some of these," I say.

"Sure," says David. "Copy whatever you need."

I borrow some more empty boxes from Katja. I return to David's office and start placing the files vertically into the boxes.

"Hey," David says, interrupting me. "What are you doing with my contracts?"

"You said I could copy them," I say.

"Copy, yeah. Pack them up, no way."

I explain that most, if not all, of his files are relevant to the lawsuit. There are too many to copy at TriCom.

"But I need those files," he whines.

"It'll just be a few days," I promise.

"Can't you give them someone else's files?"

I tell him that I'm reviewing everyone's files, and that many other files will be copied.

"And who are you?" he asks, as if he's seeing me for the first time.

"I'm a lawyer for TriCom," I say. "I'm your lawyer."

He squints at me. "How do I know that?"

It's a good question. I could be anyone off the street in a suit and tie claiming to be a lawyer. An escapee from an asylum whose bizarre fantasy is to collect legal documents.

I give him a business card. "Call my boss," I say. "Call your boss."

He shrugs off my card. "You know what I'm saying? These are my files."

"I understand."

"Who's going to put them back?"

"I can get a paralegal," I say.

"What if they lose them?"

"They won't."

"What if they do?"

I sigh. "I've been doing this for years," I lie. "I've never heard of a copy service losing files."

"We should wait for the chairman."

I make some quick calculations. I could call Eric and ask him to

counting David's files, I have gathered six boxes of documents. Plenty of files to review more closely when I return to New York, and I have not even covered half the building.

At three o'clock, as I am eating a takeout sandwich at a salesman's unoccupied desk, Katja tells me the chairman will see me.

Steven George is about five foot six, closely cropped gray hair, a bushy Stalin mustache. His name, I realize as I hear his accent, must have been shortened from something unpronounceably Russian. A former MIT professor, the beneficiary of cold war largesse, plucked from his native country by a well-meaning American university from which he bolted in the name of capitalism.

He is reading from a small pile of papers when I enter his office. "Yes?" he says distractedly.

"You wanted to see me?" I say.

He looks up. "*You* are asking to see *me*." His tone bites.

From his verb tense I cannot tell whether he is correcting or commanding me. Though I wanted to speak with him about his documents, I assumed that he called me into his office at David's prompting. The client's version, however, is always right. I explain my mission and ask him if he keeps any files and whether I might review them.

"What is the purpose of this review?" he asks.

His question stumps me. I know Eric spoke with him before my trip. He received a copy of the document request. He knows his company is being sued. What is the purpose of this interrogation?

"I'm responding to a document request," I say, taking the simplest and straightest route.

"Who is giving you permission?" he says.

Although we are both speaking English, the language barrier rises like a rampart between us. I remind him that he has talked with Eric; he has seen the request.

"You are taking our files," he says, "and then you are giving them to people who sue us."

"No," I say. "Yes."

"If you find something bad, you are giving them that, too."

"Only if we have to. We'll try to protect it if we can."

"No," he says, slapping his hand on his desk. "You are not deciding. I decide."

It takes me a moment to understand what he is suggesting. Then, next to his desk, I notice a shredder. The outrageous possibilities suddenly knife through me. Visions of Iran-contra, Oliver North, congressional hearings. Should I run out of the room, call Eric, call the judge, call for help? I sneak a peek at the basket beneath the shredder and, thankfully, it appears empty; but how long will it remain that way if I leave his office? I do not want my fledging legal career to end in ethics charges. The discovery process may not work well, it may not even work at all. But it's the law.

"No, sir," I say quietly.

He rises to his full height, barely clearing the desk. His mustache bristles. "Who questions this?" he demands.

"It's the American way," I say.

"America," he says disdainfully. "Land of the lawyers."

"Home of the free," I offer.

He squints at me. I can see the whole human range of emotion passing across his face, from his clenched jaw and scowl, to the quizzical tilt of one eyebrow, to the slightest dimpling in his opposite cheek. It's as if the thought processes in his brain are visible, the same brain that invented either the most innovative or biggest bust in software in years, and his brain is evaluating whether I've just insulted him or reminded him that the rule of law makes this country great.

He waves his arm at a file cabinet. "I have nothing. It's in there."

the shredder for years, for sensitive financial data. Anyway," he sighs, "I reiterated the importance of the document request. Compliance is not optional."

"Yes," I say.

"All this traveling has taken you away longer than we expected," he says. "I've apologized to Caroline. When you're done here, she wants to see you."

I wait for him to say something more, to give me another project, but apparently my audience has ended. My time on the road, after eighteen nights in hotels, a wallet thick with credit card receipts, a stack of old mail and dying houseplants, and a girlfriend who's probably dating another man by now, has ended. The documents have been collected, and Caroline awaits.

I have the distinct impression that Eric's happy to be rid of me.

Trial's End

The first headhunter called in June.

I was perfectly positioned for a lateral move to the small litigation boutique for whom she happened to be conducting a search, she told me. Move now, and forever I would be at peace.

How did she get my name? I wondered. Had someone reported that I was unhappy? Was I unhappy? She reassured me that the phone call was entirely random; she found my name in a Bar Association directory, and saw that shortly I would be starting my third year at C & C. Third-years, she claimed, were the most likely to jump ship.

Soon I was besieged by phone calls. Headhunters called nearly every week. I was wanted; I was desirable; I was marketable. The calls promised a future of success and good fortune. The headhunters had nothing but warm feelings about my résumé. For a Harvard guy like me, they said, the world was a special place.

Headhunters are paid by the transaction. There's no fee unless they place a lawyer at a new firm. Then the firm, not the lawyer, pays a fee equal to thirty percent of the lawyer's salary for the first year. By taking a lawyer from firm A where he's earning $120,000 to firm B where he will earn the same $120,000, a headhunter pockets $36,000 for the effort. The less time a headhunter spends with a client, the more she earns per hour. The quicker a lawyer accepts a job, the higher her hourly rate. A desperate and unhappy lawyer is her best customer.

and uniformed. The work could get better, the people more interesting. If I didn't think about it, the hours were nearly manageable. Then, like a flea in the ear, the possibilities buzzed about me. If I was marketable, I reasoned, shouldn't I market myself? Wasn't this the process of keeping my options open, the same process that brought me to law and to C & C in the first place? The worst thing that could happen was that I would be offered a job.

I had always succumbed to flattery, grabbed for whatever ring was placed before me, staggered onward drunk with greed. I wasn't going to stop now. Once begun, the job-search process took on a life of its own. Each step led inexorably toward the next. If I said yes to a headhunter, why not say yes to an interview; if I said yes to the interview, why not say yes to the job?

When confronted with the corporeality of another job, my commitment to C & C wavered like an adulterer. The possibility of being with someone else focused me on where I was. Had I been adequately trained? Was the work challenging? Did I *like* my job? If I was honest, the answer to all these questions was no. A lawyer should be arguing the merits of his case, not grappling with documents in the back of a warehouse or researching procedure in the library. Everyone must do his time on the chain gang, it's true; before Kate graduated to reading manuscripts, she was photocopying them. I, too, had gone from cataloging documents to gathering them. Soon, if I was lucky, I would end up like Barry Katz and then, eventually, Eric. But did I want to be Eric?

Partners made more money, and assigned work to associates like me, but they still toiled on the same cases and spent their Passovers faxing documents to the office. Senior associates, like Barry, got to incorporate cases found by junior associates like me into enormous memoranda. All of us labored to protect the rights of corporations while normal people were eating dinner with their families. I wasn't married; I had no children; but I couldn't see a future that included either at C & C. It was why there were so few female partners, and why I had yet to meet anyone, except for the support staff, who appeared to have a life outside work.

How *did* I get here, I wondered, and what was I doing at C & C? More important, what would I be doing as the years droned on? The more I thought about it, the more I realized there was no future for me at C & C. I wasn't Barry, or Charlie, or Caroline, or Eric, or Jensen. I didn't know what made those people survive, even thrive. But whatever it was, I just didn't have it. It was a simple realization, one that came to me gradually, but once arrived it remained, and I knew it would never leave until I did.

"You'll take the depositions," says Caroline.

"Me?" I say.

"Is that a problem?"

I have never taken a deposition. I assume Caroline knows this, though I don't tell her. I watched Charlie take and defend a dozen depositions in Detroit, but I have never spoken a word on the record.

"You'll write an outline and I'll review it," Caroline reassures me. "Don't worry, it's no big deal."

Though the Diamond Gravel case stagnated while I was in Detroit and then Boston, we have since sent out document requests and reviewed the documents that were produced. Now Caroline has scheduled depositions. The plaintiff, Target Sand & Stone, has yet to conduct any of its own discovery, though surely we will receive its discovery requests any day.

Back in my office I wonder whether Caroline has blessed me with an opportunity to acquire litigation experience, or shuffled off a task she's not anxious to perform. As I review the contract documents from Diamond Gravel, and the small folder

depositions of three Target witnesses: an engineer, a business manager, and the division supervisor. The first two were directly involved in the contract negotiations; the third is their boss, who reports to the company president. Caroline has set the deposition of the engineer first, the business manager second, and then the supervisor. In this way, she told me, I can learn something about Target's business practices before asking questions of the man who implements them.

On my desk I have a book called *Effective Deposition Strategies*. It tells me that taking a deposition is like having a conversation. When examining opposing witnesses one must make them feel comfortable, get them talking. They will forget where they are and spill the beans, all of which will be conveniently recorded on a written transcript.

It's the formal aspects of a deposition that concern me, however. How do I begin? What are the standard questions about education, background, work experience? I remember Charlie revising my outline for the Dekor depositions with specific questions about the deponent's background, which seemed incredibly neurotic at the time; but now, neurotic or not, I wish I had saved his revision. I consider asking Charlie for a copy, but I don't want to reveal my ignorance. Then I realize I can copy the questions directly from the deposition transcripts. One problem resolved. But what about objections? I am taking the deposition so I will not object, but how do I respond when the attorney for the witnesses objects?

The book tells me not to worry. Objections can only be to the "form" of the question; for example, if it's vague or ambiguous. Even then, the witness may answer the question if he understands it. Lawyers are prohibited from making "speaking objections," long objections that suggest an answer to the witness. But as I review the transcripts from the depositions in Detroit there are pages of objections and pages of responses. At times, I remember, it seemed like the lawyers were arguing the case in front of the witness.

According to the book, this is bad lawyering. But who should I believe, the book or Charlie? If I am faced with a long objection from the opposing lawyer should I ignore it and continue? If I ignore it, have I sacrificed my right to respond?

I call Julia.

"You're taking a deposition?" she asks. Two years at her firm and she's never taken one.

I am, I realize, lucky. Neither Daniel nor Jay has taken a deposition yet. In fact, few associates below their fourth year at C & C have taken depositions. Julia tells me that a senior litigation associate at her firm just made partner without *ever* having taken a deposition. At a small firm, where cases actually go to trial, this would be considered absurd. At Julia's firm, it was business almost as usual.

I tell her about Diamond, their salt problem, and my deposition anxiety. I wonder whether I should be sharing this information with an outsider. But the only facts I'm sharing are available to anyone from court documents. And the outsider is Julia, who knows more of my secrets than almost anyone. We have a common interest that protects the information from disclosure, I decide: we both share an interest in my well-being.

"Ignore him," Julia advises about my hypothetical opposing counsel.

"You've never taken a deposition."

"Then why are you asking me?"

Julia has been working closely with a former enforcement attorney from the Securities and Exchange Commission, one of the few lawyers at her firm with significant civil trial experience. That's why I'm asking her; that, and the fact that she knows everything.

"None of it is admissible," says Julia. "It's just posturing. The only objections are to form ~~~~~~~~~~~~~~~

~~~~~~ time and dragging out the deposition when the question can be answered anyway, comes to view his own lawyer as an adversary.

"I've seen a witness ignore his lawyer's instructions not to answer a question," Julia continues. "The guy was objecting so much that when a real question of privilege arose, the witness ignored it." Julia laughs as if remembering a good practical joke.

She has been trained by a master, schooled in the secrets of thwarting obstructionist counsel, yet still not taken a deposition. I, meanwhile, have been trained by Charlie, the stealth instructor, who barely acknowledges me.

"It's not brain surgery," says Julia, sighing into the phone. "You can't kill anyone if you screw up. You can't even maim them."

"Thanks," I say, "for the vote of confidence."

"Quit," says Kate. "Leave corporate law."

Another night, another restaurant. Kate's chosen this one, an organic vegetarian in TriBeCa where the streets offer up retail establishments grudgingly, as if they were state secrets.

"You can't stay at that place forever," she adds.

"What about making partner?" I ask.

"You're not the partner type."

What is the partner type, I wonder, and how can Kate spot one?

"You want a life," she continues. "These people are damaged goods. You said so yourself."

"I did?"

"You did."

As I remember, it was Kate who defended a partner's right to avoid his family and religious obligations by tying himself to the fax machine. But perhaps she wasn't defending the practice, only the man. He was doing the best he could without a gene for empathy. Kate raises a remonstrative eyebrow at me as she spears a brown square of something that purports to be bean curd.

"What else is there?" I ask.

Her fork jumps. "I hope that's a rhetorical question," she says.

At least five associates in my class have already left C & C. One quit after two months; he was rumored to have "psychological problems." Last year, an associate at another big firm leaped to his death from his apartment balcony. He tried to jump through his firm's windows, but they did not open. Associates leave their firms precipitously every day, though not always successfully.

"There's in-house," I admit. "There's a smaller firm. There's public service."

"Why did you become a lawyer?" asks Kate.

"My parents made me."

"Come on." She points her fork at me menacingly. The light pinwheels in her hazel eyes.

I sigh. I am not in the mood for confession. But Kate waits for an answer, and I know better than to keep her waiting. I tell her how law seemed a good balance between creativity and pragmatism, between poverty and great wealth, between public and private good.

"Do you still feel that way?" she asks.

"I feel like the balance has shifted."

"Whose fault is that?"

"Mine, partly. I've learned things I didn't know about myself, and about the practice of law."

"What have you learned?"

It's my turn to hold up my fork. "I feel like I'm in therapy."

"And I won't even bill you by the hour," says Kate. "Come on."

I glance at my plate for a minute, searching for my thoughts in the grains of brown rice. Then I say, "Law, at least as it's practiced at C & C, is about money, power, the pursuit of private good. Even that might be bearable, if

you to

The law firm defending Target Sand & Stone against Diamond's breach of contract claim is in a beige brick building located on the main street in the town of White Plains, New York. The building could be a bank, an apartment complex, a senior citizen center. I drive past it twice before catching the number outside and the small cursive sign that warns: *Attorneys-at-Law.*

I park my rental car in the small lot off the street. I am carrying two litigation briefcases filled with nearly every document produced by Target, the legal pleadings filed to date by both parties, my deposition outline, a copy of the New York Civil Practice Law and Rules, *Effective Deposition Strategies,* three pads of paper, a dozen black pens, six red pens, two yellow Hi-Liters, ten Post-it pads in assorted sizes, a box of paper clips, and a stapler. At least I won't be outsupplied.

I had assumed that Caroline would come with me, but she has left me to fend for myself. "You can handle it," she said, which I assumed was a blessing but could be a curse. Now if I screw up, I have only myself to blame.

The receptionist directs me upstairs to a beige conference room. The court reporter has already arrived. She has set up her stenographic machine and laptop computer at one end of the brown conference table. Because I am taking the deposition, C & C has hired the court reporter from its stable of reporting services. I do not know her, however, and we exchange cards and engage in awkward conversation about the weather, the commute, life in the suburbs, for about ten minutes until lapsing into silence.

Finally, after another ten minutes, Target's attorney, whose name is Richard Butzel, arrives. He's a tall, stoop-shouldered man, in his midforties, almost totally bald, with colorless eyes. He doesn't apologize for the delay, merely notes that his witness, the engineer, is on his way.

Butzel knows the court reporter from another case and, despite the fact that she's on C & C's dime, they chat energetically about some local incident. Like a teenager at his first dance, I pose stiffly, trying to affect one part bored nonchalance and one part world-weary wisdom. I remember Charlie gabbing amiably with opposing counsel in Detroit, which struck me as odd, given that they were adversaries. Perhaps the professional cabal runs deeper than the lawyer-client relationship. I wish I had asked Julia how I should behave. I know I cannot muster the energy to feign camaraderie.

Thirty-five minutes after the deposition is scheduled to begin, Stan Heller saunters into the conference room. He's a big man, as tall as Butzel, but forty pounds heavier. Florid face, florid tie, ill-matched jacket and slacks. He, too, knows the court reporter from some local business dealings, and they share gossip, which ends with the reporter, Heller, and Butzel exploding in laughter. I smile tightly.

"Ready?" asks Butzel, after he's had a good laugh, as if it's me who's been screwing around for the last three quarters of an hour.

"When you are," I say, my attempt at obnoxiousness.

The reporter swears in the witness, takes his address, the spelling of his name, then turns to me.

"Good morning, Mr. Heller," I say. I tell him who I am and where I work and explain that C & C represents Diamond Gravel in a lawsuit against Target Sand & Stone. "Are you aware of the facts of that lawsuit?"

"The facts?"

"The allegations."

"Allegations? How do you mean?"

"Are you aware that Diamond Gravel has brought a lawsuit against Target, claiming that Target owes Diamond money pursuant to a contract entered into ...

...

... Please wait until I've asked my question before you answer so that the court reporter here can take everything down. If you don't understand my question, please ask me to rephrase it. If you answer my question, I'm going to assume you understood it, is that agreed?"

"Objection," says Butzel.

I look up from my sheet, thrown by Butzel's interruption.

"The witness can't know what you're assuming," continues Butzel.

"Yeah," says Heller.

I want nothing more than to run out of the room and call Julia or Caroline. I've never heard of anyone objecting to preliminary instructions. I don't know what Butzel is doing. Is this some trick to conduct the entire deposition under protest?

"I'm not asking you to guess what I'm assuming," I say. "I'm just saying if you answer my questions I will assume you've understood them."

"The record will speak for itself," says Butzel.

"Are you telling me the witness can't answer my questions?" I ask. I feel like we're having a discussion about the nature of language. How do any of us know what words mean? How do we know what we know?

"You ask the questions. He will answer as best he can."

"That's all I ask."

"Fine."

"Okay." I'm not sure we've settled anything. But I don't know how else to proceed.

I finish my preliminary instructions, then move on to the background questions: education, work experience, current job. These questions take me less than forty-five minutes. Heller answers succinctly without objection from Butzel.

"As an engineer," I ask, "have you had any experience with requirements contracts?"

"Objection," says Butzel.

"Yeah," says Heller, "what do you mean by 'requirements contracts'?"

I admire the skill with which Butzel and Heller have tag-teamed me on the answer. Butzel obviously told Heller before the deposition that when he objects, it is usually because something about the question is vague or ambiguous. Heller immediately picked up on the term "requirements contract," which is an issue in this lawsuit.

"Are you familiar with contracts that obligate one party to provide all the goods or services that the other party requires?"

"Yeah, in general, yeah. But this wasn't a requirements contract."

"Move to strike."

Again, I've never seen anyone move to strike an answer in a deposition. I thought it was something lawyers did at trial. The best response, I decide, following Julia's advice, is to ignore it. "What's your understanding of a requirements contract?" I ask.

"Objection, lacks foundation."

"Mr. Heller?"

Heller looks to Butzel. "Should I answer?"

"You can answer," I reassure him.

"There's no foundation," says Butzel.

"He testified that this wasn't a requirements contract," I say.

"There was no foundation for your original question."

Foundation? My mind races. What exactly is foundation? From what I remember, it's an evidentiary requirement that questions be premised upon a factual foundation. My trusty deposition book didn't say anything about having to lay a foundation at a deposition, however.

"I'll withdraw the question," I say. "We'll come back to it." I don't want Butzel to think he's won this round.

ument before."

"Nope."

"No?"

"Nope."

From other documents I've read I know that Heller was involved in the process of hiring Diamond and drafting the contract between Diamond and Target. How could he have never seen the actual contract?

"In your job as an engineer for Target Sand & Stone, are you involved in the process of drafting contracts?"

"Yeah."

"Were you involved in the process of drafting the contract between Target and Diamond Gravel?"

"Yeah, but I never saw it."

"Just answer the question," says Butzel. "Don't volunteer information."

There's no rule against volunteering. There is a rule, however, against admonishing your own witness at a deposition. I let it pass because I'm not confident enough to warn Butzel.

"You never saw it?"

"Nope. I mean yeah, I never saw it."

"How is that possible?"

"Objection."

"I'm an engineer, not a lawyer. I don't get involved in the paper-work."

"Let me direct your attention to paragraph three."

"Objection. He just testified he never saw the document before."

"Paragraph three," I repeat.

"Objection. I'm not going to let this witness answer questions about a document he's never seen."

"Take a minute to read paragraph three," I suggest.

"Same objection. If you have a question about this witness's per-sonal knowledge, I'll let him answer. But he's not going to testify about something he knows nothing about."

"He was involved in drafting this contract," I protest.

"My objection is on the record."

"Mr. Heller," I say, "please take a look at paragraph three and tell me if you have an understanding of what the term 'minimum' means as it is used in that paragraph."

"I'm sorry," Heller says. "I've never seen this contract before. I have no personal knowledge. I can't testify about something I've never seen."

You have to admire a witness who picks up on all the buzzwords fed to him by his attorney. And you have to be frustrated, as I am all that morning and afternoon, by the attorney's sprinkling of ob-stacles like children's toys littering the clean path toward liability.

Name, rank, and serial number. As to everything else, Heller lacks personal knowledge. My only hope, I think as I drive back to Man-hattan, is that Caroline will not bother to read the transcript.

The discovery deadline imposed by the court in the Diamond Gravel case was rapidly approaching, and still we had not received any re-quests for documents or depositions from Target. Caroline attrib-uted it to some master plan hatched by the fiendish Richard Butzel, Esq. But I attributed it to other factors.

By the third deposition I realized that Butzel's objections were inappropriate and unfounded. While my deposition techniques were admittedly shaky, Butzel had no basis on which to instruct a witness not to answer a question if it didn't involve an attorney-client privilege, and I told him so. He mumbled and muttered about my inappropriate questions, but ultimately allowed the witness to answer questions about his understanding of the contract.

more hours reviewing them with Caroline, and still more hours revising and reorganizing them, Butzel seemed to have spent exactly five minutes preparing his witnesses. In fact, at the last deposition, when I asked the division supervisor whether he had a chance to meet with his attorney before the deposition, a standard question to establish for the record that a witness was prepared so as to avoid any disclaimers at trial, the supervisor said that he had not. He spoke with Butzel's secretary about the time and place, and saw Butzel for a minute outside the conference room, but had never spoken with him in preparation for the deposition. After the weeks Charlie and I had spent with our witnesses in Detroit, I was stunned by the answer. Butzel seemed unperturbed, as if it were his standard operating procedure, which it probably was.

Whatever the reasons, Butzel operated by his shoestrings. Perhaps he thought the Diamond Gravel case would never go to trial. Maybe he knew it would but didn't care. Most likely, he reasoned that he could get the documents he needed at trial and examine the witnesses on the stand. That was his first mistake, but not his last.

The bleating phone jolts me from sleep. I fumble for my clock, thinking it's the alarm, until, after four rings, the answering machine picks up. I hear Caroline's voice and lift the phone to interrupt her midsentence.

"I hope I didn't wake you," she says.

It's nine A.M. Just late enough to excuse her. It's also Sunday. What's her excuse?

The discovery deadline is Monday, she reminds me. She wants to pin Target down, make certain they can't seek alternative means of discovery. What am I doing right now? Can I come in to the office?

I know she's not asking. I tell her I'll be there in half an hour. She says she'll meet me.

"What's with her?" asks Kate as I dress.

"You don't want to know," I say.

In the cab ride to the office I wonder why Caroline needs me today. Tomorrow, when discovery closes, nothing magic will happen. We won't turn into pumpkins. But still, Caroline needs me today.

The security guard doesn't even look at me as I walk past him and wait for the elevator. I rise nonstop to the twenty-eighth floor. The floor is deserted; I have beaten all the weekend warriors into the office. I unlock my door, turn on my lights, and step inside. There are no messages on my voice mail, no pink slips by the telephone.

Now what?

Without clearer instructions from Caroline, I realize there's nothing I can do. I turn on my computer, that takes sixty seconds, and then sit back at my desk. I don't have a specific research project. All I know is that Caroline wants to prevent Target from trying to make an end run around the discovery deadline. I pick up a copy of the *New York Civil Practice Law and Rules,* the procedural bible for New York State courts. I flip through the discovery sections, half-hoping to see something that says *failure to make timely discovery*. But no such luck.

I look at the phone, urging it to ring. When it doesn't, I pick it up and call Julia at home. No one answers. I hang up before the answering machine finishes its recorded message. I turn back to my computer. For the next hour I set several high scores on Mine-Sweeper.

At eleven-fifteen Caroline appears in my doorway. Her hair looks freshly cut; it gleams like obsidian beneath the lights. Her blue eyes shimmer like glaciers.

"What'd you find?" she asks.

I fumble to close the MineSweeper screen. "I'm not sure what we're looking for," I admit.

Instead, the client pays now for what it might not have to pay for later.

"He could serve those requests tomorrow," she says. "I want to be ready to go to the judge."

Poor Butzel, he doesn't know what he's up against. Or maybe he does. Caroline has never gone to trial. Butzel has tried dozens of cases, most of them, as he was fond of reminding me during breaks in the depositions, without assistance from "kiddie lawyers" like me. In the courtroom, what he lacks in preparation he'll make up in experience. It's we who won't stand a chance.

"When do you want this?" I ask.

"Yesterday," says Caroline.

I wait for her to smile, to acknowledge the cliché. But she turns and walks out, leaving the smell of expensive shampoo in her wake.

"He did it," my telephone squawks.

I know who it is and who she means and what he did even as I hold the receiver from my ear.

"I said he would and he did," Caroline says.

There's nothing like being right, I think, except telling other people how right you are.

My research over the weekend indicated the best way to respond to any belated discovery requests from Butzel was informally, with a letter to the judge. While we could ignore his request, and force him to make a motion, we decided late on Sunday night that if Butzel served us with discovery we would request a judicial conference. This would speed the case along and let the judge know we were prepared for trial. Delay was Butzel's only tactic and, for the first time, our enemy.

Caroline, however, wants to revisit our decision. She's brought Eric into the equation. Can I come to her office for a conference?

While Diamond is Eric's client, Caroline has handled almost all aspects of the litigation. At $100 an hour less than Eric, it's simple math. But now, on a trivial discovery issue, where the procedure is straightforward and unremarkable, Caroline has turned to her tutor.

When I arrive at Caroline's office, I see that Eric has a copy of the memorandum I wrote at two in the morning, and a stack of cases, many of which he has highlighted in yellow marker. His thoroughness comes with a price, however, and he's not throwing in a toaster. As the three of us discuss the issue, a silent cash register rings: thirteen dollars every minute.

"The rules require a response," says Eric. "The response triggers his time to move." He means that before a party serving a discovery request can move to compel a response, the party upon whom the requests are served must object.

"But these requests are too late," says Caroline.

"You can't invoke the authority of the court without a procedural mechanism."

"What if we ignored the requests?"

"He could move under the rules to compel a response."

"So maybe we should wait for him to move?"

"There's the danger of waiving our objections if we fail to respond, even if the requests are untimely."

And so on, and so forth. I listen to their argument with an ear to the amount of work involved. A letter to the judge would be the simplest remedy, and the least amount of work. Objecting to the discovery requests would require an analysis of each request. It would also require someone, probably Jackie, to retype each request and our response. Whichever option we choose, I know Eric will want immediate action. Caroline will want it yesterday.

"You'd have to consider the waiver argument," Eric is saying, "but it's the safest course."

Fifteen minutes and $195 later, not including the time it took Eric

[text obscured] She means tonight, and she means me.

"What else are you working on?" Eric asks me.

My résumé, I think, but I tell him that Dekor is relatively calm. There's always something to do for TriCom—the last crisis was a defamatory press release, courtesy of Steven George, that blasted the plaintiffs for bringing the lawsuit, which Charlie defused with research assistance from me—but nothing Daniel can't handle.

"Good," he says. "We need to look at the waiver issue."

I worked all weekend to reach a conclusion which, on Monday, has been tossed aside like a broken kite. They could have had their strategy session on Friday, before Caroline called me in to research yesterday's idea.

"You'll do the first draft," Caroline says to me after Eric has left her office. "We should try to get it out tonight."

There are twenty-five requests for documents and eighteen interrogatories. While I have seen Charlie's responses to discovery requests, I have never drafted a response myself. Eric decreed that we couldn't just make a blanket objection to the timeliness of the requests. We must examine each separately and object on as many grounds as possible. In addition, there's the research on the question of whether we waive our right to object to the timeliness of the discovery requests if we respond to them, which could take most of the day. I don't see how I can do everything before tomorrow.

"Tell Word Processing to leave a draft on my chair in the morning," says Caroline, as if it were a simple matter of typing. "I'll make the final changes."

Spiraling down the staircase to my office, I decide that Caroline's order is a deadline, not a vote of confidence in my abilities.

As I considered the possibility of leaving C & C, I began to see my experiences through that critical lens. I remembered the first time I worked with Caroline, cataloging documents for a database in the Consolidated litigation. I was both overqualified for the job, yet cast loose without direction. The job itself was a combination of over- and underpreparation: the cataloging should have been done years earlier, yet it was unnecessary. As with the most recent Diamond Gravel research, I worked needlessly all weekend because of Caroline's thoughtlessness.

I remembered the countless hours I spent in the library researching legal issues for Barry Katz and other senior associates who rarely, if ever, used my research. I remembered the document production in Detroit, where I was trapped in an overheated and airless warehouse pulling papers from former employees' files, and the document production at TriCom where clients viewed me as their adversary. In both cases, although I had undoubtedly learned how to produce documents in response to a document request, I couldn't see the larger point of the exercise. The lawyers bombarded each other with requests and objections, motions to compel and, ultimately, boxes of documents that were dutifully filed by paralegals and forgotten. The process was anything but a search for truth; rather, it simply shifted power to the side with more resources to resist. In the old days, businesses kept their secrets locked in their drawers; now they hired lawyers to do it.

I remembered the summary judgment motion and the motion to compel in Tricom. These motions had swallowed hundreds of hours, not just mine but Daniel's and Charlie's and Eric's, and we weren't even successful. But outcome aside, I might have learned something meaningful if Charlie had sat down with me and critiqued my efforts on the summary judgment draft, or if I had done anything more than check citations and arrange for our opposition to the motion to compel to be copied and bound. The skills I had learned were necessary for big-firm practice, but I did not want to practice law where form swallowed substance, where responsibility was bestowed

my cases. But I had made one decision, and they had made another.

Most of all, I remembered the coldness of law firm life. The contempt with which Charlie held younger associates. Caroline's unfocused assignments. Jensen's fair-weathered support. I remembered Jay's competitiveness and Daniel's inhuman work schedule. I remembered the difficulty of trying to have a life outside work, the insanity of my running schedule, the lengths I had to go to do something I loved. The late nights, lost weekends, conference room dinners. What I didn't remember were any close friendships I had forged, any attempt among the lawyers to connect. The only people toward whom I felt any warmth were not even lawyers.

Was there something wrong with me? I wondered. Was I simply a malcontent, a dreamer, a whiner, a naif? Was there something wrong with C & C? Or was there something wrong with the law?

I spent my last all-nighter at C & C drafting responses to Butzel's belated discovery requests. Caroline gave me several sample responses from other cases, and I copied, cut, pasted, and invented responses based on those. Jackie worked with me late into the night and, when she gave up, Sam relieved her. Both were their usual human, unflappable selves, and I realized, sadly, that they were my closest friends at C & C.

It wasn't the law. It couldn't be the law. I wouldn't allow myself to believe the law was to blame. I had read enough political theory to know how Marx postulated that a capitalist economy alienated man from the product of his labor. Law was just another job where the worker felt disconnected from his work. But law, particularly as it was practiced at C & C and other big corporate firms, was also unique among capitalist enterprises. It produced no goods, rarely addressed substantive issues, almost never provided closure, pitted lawyers against each other in the struggle for partnership, isolated lawyers in the library and their offices, tended to weed out the sociable and genial. All these factors, and undoubtedly others, contributed to the unhappiness I felt at C & C.

The morning after my all-nighter, when the discovery responses were safely in Caroline's hands, I committed myself to leaving C & C. If I had learned anything in two years, I knew that making partner would not change the nature of the work or the environment. The clues had been there all along, since my summer associate days, but money, inertia, and a deliberate ignorance created false hopes. To be fair, until I did the job, I could never adequately critique it; secondhand observation and well-intentioned warnings do not substitute for experience.

I made it my daily assignment to send out at least one résumé, to make one phone call to someone who knew someone who might be looking for someone like me. Most of the résumés went unanswered; most of the calls were dead ends. But the more time passed, the greater my commitment grew, and my certainty that big-firm practice was not for me. The irony was that without C & C on my résumé, I would never have heard from a headhunter, never have gotten the interviews I did, and never found another job. Even a Harvard imprimatur could not convince a company to hire an untried litigator for their legal staff. Most private-sector employers expected several years at a big law firm before they would even touch you.

Illusion, as always, was everything. A lawyer who worked at a small firm trying personal injury cases in court had far more experience than I. Yet no headhunters called that lawyer, while I had to invent excuses to keep the headhunters away. Employers said they wanted experience, but what they really wanted were lawyers who looked like them and had done the same thing they had. The circle was complete: law students went to big firms because everyone said they would get good experience; the experience they got was good because everyone said it was. The emperor said he had clothes, and so he did.

We drove to the hearing in White Plains in Caroline's Lexus. On the drive back to the office, I drew stick figures on the air-conditioned window while Caroline spoke to Eric on the car phone.

The trial would be held before the judge, not a jury, because neither side had requested a jury trial. We had witnesses to prepare, pretrial motions to write, opening and closing arguments. Caroline had not yet said which witnesses would be mine, but I silently hoped for the comptroller, a burly, humorous man with a loquacious manner. Maybe I could even make the opening argument. Before a judge, rather than a jury, an opening argument would be similar to an argument on a summary judgment motion with none of the theatrics of a jury trial. It would be a legal argument, and I believed I could do it.

Though I had spent time on various emergencies in the TriCom case, such as the defamatory press release, I was averaging about twenty hours a week on Diamond Gravel. At that rate, over the next few months, my time on trial preparation would cost Diamond about $30,000. Caroline spent less time on the case, but her billing rate was higher; I guessed her charges were about the same. Eric, too, was putting in some hours behind the scenes, despite his delegation of the case to Caroline. All told, I estimated that trial preparation would cost Diamond about $75,000. That was in addition to the $100,000 already spent on the case, and $50,000 that would be spent on the actual trial. If Diamond recovered the $600,000 it claimed from Target, Diamond would owe C & C about a third, the same amount as if C & C had handled the case on a contingency fee.

The first task was to prepare a pretrial memorandum of law, spotlighting for the judge the important legal issues to address before and during the trial. Next was to collect all the exhibits we intended to introduce to support our case. Finally, we should organize and outline the trial testimony of our witnesses. Caroline gave me these jobs as we pulled into a garage near C & C. Like all my work with Caroline, the orders were vague and ill-defined. She spoke rapidly, phrasing the issues so broadly as to be practically meaningless; for example, "What do we have to prove?" But for once, I didn't mind. I was going to trial. I would take what I could get, and I would love it.

Over the next two months, as we prepared for trial, I had five job interviews for in-house litigation positions. While the degrees of responsibility in each position varied, all promised to bring me into court and to give me control of a significant caseload. All were with corporations involved in the entertainment industry, broadly defined: companies that produced music, television shows, computer games, books, movies, videos. After each interview, I felt a great surge of energy. The process of asking the interviewers questions about their jobs and listening to them describe what sounded like real, and interesting, work inspired me to want to do the work.

The odds, I knew, were against me. One interviewer showed me a stack of thirty résumés she had received that day. There were more than three hundred in a pile behind her. Once I waited awkwardly with two other applicants to see the same interviewer. Another time, an applicant was still being interviewed as I was led into the office by a secretary. The world had changed since I graduated from law school; or, rather, it had shrunk. I was no longer interviewing for one of fifty jobs. I was interviewing for one. Still, I had gotten these interviews, I told myself, which was better than ninety percent of the other candidates.

Through it all, I attempted to guard my privacy. I didn't share my job search with anyone but Kate and Julia. I tried to make interviews during the lunch hour when I wouldn't be missed. I composed my letters and résumés at home, although I read the classifieds at the office. Before, when people left C & C, it seemed like a spur-of-the-

tainly satisfied my end of the bargain. The firm wanted us to be part of the team, or at least participate in tryouts. But really there were two teams, or more, and I had to do what was best for mine. I knew if the situation were reversed, few would feel guilty about me.

"Childs is ready," Caroline announces, as if he were dinner.

Two months later nothing has changed, and yet everything has changed. Charlie is writing a summary judgment motion in the De-kor Industries case without my assistance because, according to him, of my obligations to Caroline. TriCom's board of directors has been fired by Steven George and replaced by a new board of insiders. Daniel and I are researching the application of the attorney-client privilege to former, and potentially adverse, employees. My last case is ready for trial.

"We're going to prep him at my apartment over the weekend," she adds.

Childs is Diamond Gravel's comptroller. Though I have prepared a list of questions for his direct examination, and gathered all the exhibits that he will authenticate so we can introduce them into evidence, Caroline has still not told me that he is my witness. In fact, she has not yet given me any witnesses. With the trial merely a week away, I should know whom I'm examining in order to prepare. I won't let myself believe that Caroline has changed her mind.

"Whose witness is he?" I ask.

Caroline frowns. We're standing near the elevator banks. She's going home early. I'm staying late. She claims to be working at her Fifth Avenue apartment. I can fax her anything she needs.

"I'm sorry," she says, and she seems genuinely contrite. "I know I promised you a witness."

Actually, she promised to share the trial responsibilities, but I don't say anything.

"We just can't do it," she continues. "Childs is the client. I know it would be great experience. . . ." She lets her voice trail off.

Of course I understand. I knew it was too much to hope for. No big firm would let a third-year associate share a trial. Why did I even think Caroline would keep her promise? If I screwed up in front of Childs, or in front of anyone for that matter, it would look as if C & C were training associates at the expense of the client. Never mind that Caroline and I have the same amount of trial experience, namely zero, never mind that the client might actually want the less expensive lawyer to take some of the less important witnesses to keep costs down, never mind that I might stay at C & C if I had more opportunities to do real work, Caroline has made her decision.

"It's not my choice," she says. "It's Eric's client."

I tell her not to worry; it's not a big deal. I say good-bye as the elevator closes and sweeps her down thirty-one flights. I've had my fifth interview this week. I believe it's only a matter of time. Caroline has simply made it easier.

I spend the night in Daniel's office, listening to CDs and preparing trial exhibits. I sit on the floor while Daniel works on another re-search project for Jensen. We are not friends, exactly, but I find his presence reassuring, and I trust him. "I told you so," he says when I tell him about the trial. I don't remember him telling me anything, but if it makes him happy I won't disagree.

Already I am thinking about the people I will miss, and oddly, despite himself, I think I will miss Daniel.

*   *   *

The next morning I'm at Caroline's apartment by nine. Eric is already there, but Childs is not. Caroline helps her nanny feed breakfast to her son while Eric and I sit in the living room reading documents, deposition transcripts, and the newspaper. We are here, rather than at the office, because this is where Caroline prefers to

and tastefully furnished with muted fabrics and fine furniture. On one wall, there is an oil portrait of Caroline, her husband, and their son.

I wonder why Eric has arrived so early, if he plans to stay all day, and if the client is paying for his assistance.

Childs arrives exactly at ten, which, apparently, is the time Caroline told him to arrive. I have been reading the newspaper for most of that time, at a cost to the client of $200 per hour, my new billing rate as a third-year associate. I could have been home sleeping while Caroline fed her son, I think, a better proposition for all except C & C's bottom line.

I've spoken with Childs on the phone, but in person he's even more likable. Physically, he's unremarkable: average height, slightly overweight, brown hair, brown eyes. But he speaks wonderfully: his business school vocabulary overlaid with a heavy Brooklyn accent. He says, "Deze receivables," and "Doze liabilities." By the end of the morning, we are all infected with his mannerisms.

The goal here is to establish that Diamond Gravel did not save money by not delivering the salt. Their costs are essentially the same whether they delivered one ton or one thousand tons of salt. The bulk of Diamond's operations are sunk in fixed costs: equipment, machinery, labor. They can't fire people if it snows less because they never know what tomorrow might bring. They can't refine less salt because they have to be prepared. They already own the trucks to transport the salt. City plows actually spread the salt on the road. The only real savings to Diamond are fuel costs when their trucks don't have to drive from the plant to Target with more salt, and certain incidentals.

"Deze contracts are pure profit," Childs says.

How about dem contracts? I want to ask.

We've been through much of this before with Childs, but because he was never deposed we never had to prepare his story. Caroline and Eric take him step by step through his testimony. They don't actually give him the questions they will ask, or his answers, but that's only because they don't want his responses to sound canned. Short of that, they essentially tell him how to answer.

"Then I'm going to ask you about operations at the plant," says Caroline. "Tell me a little bit about the refining of salt."

"You got your different kinds of salt," says Childs. "You wouldn't put our salt on your food."

"But the quantity you refine doesn't depend on the weather, does it?"

"That's true."

"It depends on your contractual obligations."

"Yeah."

"So tell us about that."

"Every year we estimate our production based on the guarantees in our contracts."

"By 'guarantees' you mean the minimum quantities that your contracts with various contractors obligate you to deliver?"

"Yeah."

"So let's try that answer again."

Caroline orders a late lunch. Childs expresses his gratitude for such a delicious spread. I wonder if he knows he's paying for it. Around four, Eric leaves. At five, Caroline calls it a day. Same time tomorrow, she instructs. She doesn't say whether that means nine or ten, and I'm afraid to ask. Instead, I arrive at nine. Childs arrives at ten. Eric beats us both.

*   *   *

The trial took three days. Each day I met Caroline at her apartment at 7:30 and we drove to White Plains together. Besides Childs, Diamond's other witnesses were the president of the company and the head of operations whom we had prepped in the office during the

ation and then deliver no salt if Target didn't need it. Yes, said the supervisor. Even the judge looked incredulous. Heller, the engineer whom I had deposed, miraculously remembered that the quantity specified in the contract was not a guarantee; it was an estimate and not binding on the parties. When Caroline confronted him with his deposition testimony, in which he said he had no personal knowledge of the contract language and couldn't testify about it, Heller just shrugged; he hadn't remembered what he knew at the time, he claimed. As for Diamond's witnesses, Butzel couldn't touch them.

At the end of the trial, Caroline argued for two alternative recoveries. Either give Diamond the entire value of the contract, which was what it bargained for, or give it the value of the contract minus its saved costs. The judge said he would issue an opinion shortly.

Caroline was not terrible. But she was not great. She was nervous, which was to be expected, but she also flubbed some easy questions. At one point, she committed the cardinal sin of cross-examination, asking Heller "Why?" in reponse to an answer. "Why?" allows a witness on cross-examination to wrest control from the examining attorney and expand upon his answer, when the point of cross-examination is to keep tight control of a witness by restricting his answers to yes or no. Even I had read this in a book.

Despite the unknown, the trial was not a terrifying experience. We made mistakes, but the judge accommodated them: he led us through the formalities of introducing documents into evidence; he examined some of the witnesses himself; he overruled many objections to the relevance of certain questions. Because there was no jury, the judge was not concerned about prejudice. Let the lawyers put on their case; he would weed through the chaff and find the kernels of truth. Though I was mostly a passive observer—handing Caroline documents when she needed them, pointing her to relevant sections of deposition testimony, carrying the briefcases—what I witnessed was enough to convince me that in a different legal setting, where I was in court more often and confronting the merits of cases rather than the procedural grind, my work would be more meaningful.

After final arguments, Butzel made a halfhearted settlement offer on the courthouse steps. One hundred fifty thousand dollars in settlement of all claims. Caroline said she had no authority to accept the offer, but she was certain the client would reject it. In fact, she knew Diamond would not take less than $450,000 to settle the case. But by pretending she needed to consult her client, she preserved the illusion of reasonableness, casting her client in the "bad cop" role. Later, she could come back wearing the mantle of conciliation and try to extract more money from Target. It's not me, she could say, it's my crazy client. The fear of an intractable client often increased settlement offers. Negotiation was a game of chicken. If the other side believed you wouldn't move, it would move sooner than face the oncoming train.

But for Target, it was too little, too late. It had wandered along the tracks with its legs shackled to the rails. Now as the train bore down, no amount of fancy footwork could save it.

Epilogue

When the job offer arrives, in the form of a telephone call from the deputy general counsel, I am mired in deposition preparation in the TriCom case. The plaintiffs' attorneys have cast their nets widely, subpoenaing employees and former employees across the country. Someone will have to prepare witnesses from Takoma to Fort Worth to Gainesville to Boston.

Someone, but not me.

How can I explain my feeling of freedom as I accept the in-house position? I feel as if I've been filled with movement, lifted lighter than air. I've seized control from my masters for just a moment and spun my servitude into freedom. It's like waking up one morning and realizing you have no feelings for the woman who's been tearing at your heart for years, and you've fallen in love again.

The first person I tell at C & C is Jackie.

"I knew it," she says. "All those closed doors and secret phone calls."

I didn't know anyone noticed, but of course Jackie would.

"They all leave. Story of my life." She shrugs resignedly.

I hold out my hand to shake hers, but as she approaches I realize she intends to hug or, worse, kiss me. I have never touched Jackie.

We are in my office, with the door partially closed. Anyone can see us. But there's no stopping her. Her bracelets and hoops jangle as she wraps her thin and surprisingly strong arms around my back, then plants a kiss on my cheek.

"Don't be a stranger," she says. Then she lets me go. And I go.

The next person I tell should be a partner, I know, someone in charge. There are really only three partners with whom I've exchanged more than just a few pleasantries: the assigning partner, Jensen, and Eric. I decide to tell Eric because he feels most like my "boss," and let him spread the word.

Outside his office the usual queue of associates wait as if for a sold-out concert. I take a number and trudge patiently forward. Though I asked Jackie to keep a secret until I told Eric, I know she won't. I hope that firm gossip moves slower than I do.

Finally, Eric's secretary grants me a five-minute audience. "He has a conference call at one," she warns as she escorts me to the door. Then she retreats to the perimeter of her cubicle.

I am alone with the man.

"Eric," I begin. My prepared speech tumbles out. I hear myself saying the words "good experience," "miss the people," "difficult decision," "a great opportunity." When I finish, Eric is smiling, though his eyes are on one of his laptops.

"Wonderful news," he says. He seems genuinely happy, and I feel the breath return to my lungs. He'll miss me, of course, but he understands my decision. No one owns associates; they just rent them.

The phone rings, his conference call. He smiles again, my audience ended. He promises to discuss my bright future over lunch. He's certain we'll have the opportunity to work together again. Then he enters something into his computer while the other hand answers the telephone. I backsprint out of the room.

The gossip has spread faster than voicemail. First Jay, then Daniel, come into my office.

"You bastard," says Jay.

I thank him for his kind words.

"Don't feel bad about abandoning us."

I understand that I've been medevacked to safety, my Purple Heart intact, while my buddies fight snapping turtles in the killing fields. A giddy survivor's guilt tickles me: half pleasure, half pain.

know. Perhaps, neither will he.

Mary appears at the door. Her face looks swollen and puffy, as if she has been crying.

"Have you heard?" she says to Daniel and Jay with the secret and perverse glee of someone sharing news of a cancer or an earthquake.

If Mary knows, the security guard in the lobby probably knows by now, too.

"What will we do?" she says. "You're one of my favorite associates."

Her favorite associate? How, I wonder, does she treat her disfavored associates?

"I thought I was your favorite associate," says Jay.

"You, too," Mary says. "You all are. And then you leave."

For a moment, I feel a twinge of sympathy for Mary. Each year she learns fifty or sixty new names, only to have them forget hers. She's the perennial mother, constantly losing her children.

"Get over it," says Daniel.

She squints at him from beneath the penny-colored bangs of her wig. "I will," she says, "when you leave."

The rest of the day is a parade of associates coming to pay their respects. After congratulating me, many of them want to learn how I got the job. Did I know someone? Did I use a headhunter? They, too, are looking for an in-house position. If I hear of anything . . .

At six-thirty I decide to visit Kate. I have not left this early since my first day at C & C. Though I won't be starting my new job for over a month, and there's plenty of work to do before then, I grant myself a small personal celebration.

As I shrug into my suit jacket, Caroline slips into the room and shuts the door behind her.

I have feared this confrontation all day. Though the judge has not issued a decision in the Diamond Gravel case, there will undoubtedly be an appeal no matter who wins. My absence will mean more work for her; bringing another associate up to speed will take time. I also fear a sour note in a sweet day. I have heard nothing but good wishes; I do not want someone to tell me I am making a mistake.

The door clicks. I force myself to look at her. At first I think it's an allergy; only when she begins to speak do I realize she's crying.

"We'll miss you," she says. "I'll miss you. We worked so well together." Her throat makes a sound like swallowing molasses. Then she comes behind my desk and hugs me.

I mumble vague words of encouragement and good cheer. In truth, I am stunned. After nearly three years, after the ruined weekends, the late nights, the broken promises, she is sad to see me go. She thinks we worked so well together, but I don't remember working with her, just for her. Until this moment I wasn't even sure she liked me.

"I'm sorry," she says as she backs away and wipes at her eyes with her jacket sleeve. Then she laughs, her white and perfect teeth like jewelry. "I get emotional," she explains.

It's a natural reaction, I tell her. But life at C & C is anything but natural. In the state of nature, human beings share work, not delegate; they praise rigorous effort, not take it for granted; they live and work in close proximity, not separated by partitions and doors; their labor has meaning and substance, not futility; they are kind instead of poor, nasty, brutish, and short.

"I just wonder how I'm going to survive without you," she says with a small smile, a slight flirtation, the first recognition of my humanity.

"You'll find a way," I say.

And she will.

My farewell party was held on a Wednesday evening in the thirty-fifth-floor conference room. As a pale sun set over the Hudson, cast-

look back. Jackie kicked him in the shins. Though Charlie did not make an appearance, Jensen did. He sidled up to me at the bar to wish me good luck. He was sorry we had not had the opportunity to work together, but perhaps we would in the future. Eric, too, managed to plug C & C's excellent reputation as outside counsel to America's major corporations.

I realized that, for C & C, this was not a moment of sadness, but a moment of rejoicing. Each associate who left the firm for a corporation's legal department, as I did, was perfectly positioned to direct work to C & C when the corporation needed counsel. Though the firm lost the billable hours I generated, they were easily replaced by next year's crop of associates. Meanwhile, C & C planted the spores from which new work would grow. This explained the good cheer, the promises of future lunch dates, the expensive hors d'oeuvres and open bar, the happy feelings. I was not rejecting the C & C family; I was expanding it.

There would be others like me, associates who departed while they still had a choice. Between their third and fifth years over half the associates would leave. It was so much more civilized this way; a mutual leave-taking rather than a unilateral one. C & C didn't really want us to stay. Why should they? Most of us were competent; few were brilliant; none generated new business. Where we trod, a new associate would soon cover our tracks. The partners would have been happy with zero growth in the partnership, a steady stream of profits, an unending and fluid source of associates. The only reason to keep making new partners was to keep attracting associates, the income-generating base of the pyramid. A firm that made no new partners would soon be shunned by law students at the top schools. Though we knew, statistically, that our struggles were exercises in futility, we didn't want our faces rubbed in it. We were goal-oriented; the illusion had to be preserved.

As the light left the earth, glasses were raised and toasts were made. Caroline presented me with two farewell gifts: a leather brief-case with my name embossed below the initials C & C; and my year-end bonus, $15,000.

Thus did my days at Crowley & Cavanaugh come to their appointed and foreseen end. Not with a bang, or even a whimper, but with a hearty handshake and best wishes for a mutually profitable and eternal acquaintance. Because you can't ever really leave your family, you see, no matter how dysfunctional; they will find you in the pages of an alumni directory, a legal symposium, a guide to practitioners. They will stop you on the subway one sultry evening and inquire after your new wife, your new job, your new apartment. They don't forget; nor will you.

In the years to come I would see my experiences at Crowley & Cavanaugh each time as if anew. Sometimes embittered, sometimes laughable, sometimes a necessary rite of passage. The choices I made, the options I opened and closed, the place where my decisions had taken me. I am here because of C & C. The pleasure I find in supervising my own cases, my frustration at the pace of discovery, the thrill of the open courtroom, the continual dancing around the merits, all because of how I traveled. In the parallel universe where another life I could have led lives, there is a young man who did not graduate into the practice of big-firm law. I wonder if he is happy.